ISRAEL'S
BIBLE LANDS

ISRAEL'S BIBLE LANDS

A Walk Through the Past

O. Preston Robinson and Christine H. Robinson

Published by
DESERET BOOK COMPANY
1973

LIBRARY CONGRESS CATALOG CARD
No. 73-88233

ISBN No. 0-87747-023-5

Copyright 1973

by

DESERET BOOK COMPANY

Lithographed by

DESERET PRESS

in the United States of America

Foreword

TO the people of Israel the Bible is both a statement of faith and a history. In both capacities it is taught in our schools whose pupils regularly make outings to locations like Samson's birthplace in the Judean hills, Solomon's stables at Megiddo and Mount Tabor in the north, Tiberias and Capernaum on the Sea of Galilee, Gath, Ashkelon, and many others in the south. The lessons are taught in the tongue of Abraham, Moses, David, and the Prophets which is today again the language of the land. The modern children of Israel walk in the steps of their past, and through this association continually renew the faith of their fathers.

Thousands of Israelis, including political leaders, professors, army officers, members of the clergy as well as laymen, discuss regularly and share newly found knowledge of the Bible in large gatherings as well as in small study groups. The annually held Bible Contest, in which prizes are awarded for knowledge of the Book of Books, is closely followed by all sections of the population, with an interest matched only by that given to major archaeological expeditions. These two spheres are of intense interest to the present day Israeli, who looks to the future with a sound knowledge of the past.

The archaeological research which has been undertaken with vigor since the establishment of the State of Israel has rescued from the dust of history great monuments of the past, many of which are of major significance to Christianity, and Israel's people have assumed with pride the custodial responsibilities incumbent upon them as the people of the Book. The Bible is to the Jew, as it is to the Christian, a living and vital entity.

It is with pleasure, therefore, that we greet those who come and visit us and share in this revitalization through personal association.

To the readers of this book, so ably written by Dr. and Mrs. Robinson, I extend an invitation to see for themselves, and assure them of a most sincere and cordial welcome.

Theodore Kollek
Mayor, Jerusalem, Israel

v

THE little strip of land known as Palestine is an extremely fascinating, interesting and historical spot. Into this small area is packed a remarkable share of drama, history, intrigue, hope, and contention.

The Holy Land, or Bible Land as this country is known to countless millions, is the birthplace of two great world religions and the area of development of another. The Hebrews and the Christians both place the origins of their faiths here and Islam, which had its birth nearby, grew up and matured in this rugged little country. This is the land of Abraham, Isaac, and Jacob, and of Moses and Joshua, and of the Old Testament judges, kings, and prophets. It is the land of Jesus of Nazareth and of his disciples, Peter, James, John, and Paul.

Some of history's most violently fought wars erupted in this drama-packed area. Here the Egyptians, Babylonians, Assyrians met and battled. The area was invaded by Alexander the Great, by the Romans, the crusaders, the Moslems, the Turks, and the British.

Today, this country is a land of amazing contrasts. Probably in no other place in the world do the ancient and the modern mingle so intimately. Here, only a few miles from beautiful, modern cities, one can visit Bedouin tents where Nomads live much as they did at the time of Abraham. In one field one sees oxen, led by veiled women, pulling ancient plows while in the next a modern tractor turns the soil. Dotted on the crest of numerous hills are crusaders' castles and forts. In the now excavated ruins, one can visit Canaanite altars, Hittite communities and Philistine strongholds. At old Jericho, the visitor may walk around, over and through the walls that Joshua's faith brought tumbling down.

Israel's Bible Lands is the result of an insatiable interest and four recent visits to this dramatically interesting country. The authors hope this book will stimulate the imaginations of readers and motivate them to expand their interest and knowledge about this most fascinating and important section of our shrinking world.

Since the six-day war of June 1967, most of the Bible sites are now under the control of the Israelis. Although not all of the areas where important Bible events occurred are covered in this book, most of the important sites are presented. Due to the importance of Jerusalem, the significant biblical sites in this most interesting city are presented first. The chapters which follow are then arranged alphabetically. The only area not entirely in Israel, described in this book, is the Decapolis. Due to the magnificence of the ruins of Jerash, one of these splendid cities, the authors felt impressed to present background and pictures of this spectacular and most interesting additional Bible area.

O. P. R.
C. H. R.

Contents

Illustrations

x

The Bible Land

a brief historical background

A general view of the city of Jerusalem as it looks today.

"O Jerusalem, that bringeth good tidings, lift up thy voice with strength; lift it up, be not afraid; say unto the cities of Judaea, Behold your God." (Isaiah 40:9.)

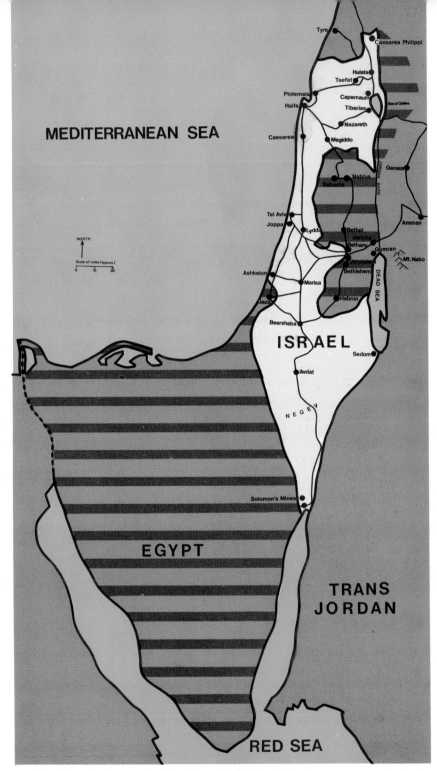

Israel today showing the border which divided the country after the 1948 war and the area (striped) obtained by Israel during the 1967 six-day war.

The Bible Land

a brief historical background

A general view of the city of Jerusalem as it looks today.

"O Jerusalem, that bringeth good
tidings, lift up thy voice with
strength; lift it up, be not afraid;
say unto the cities of Judaea,
Behold your God." (Isaiah 40:9.)

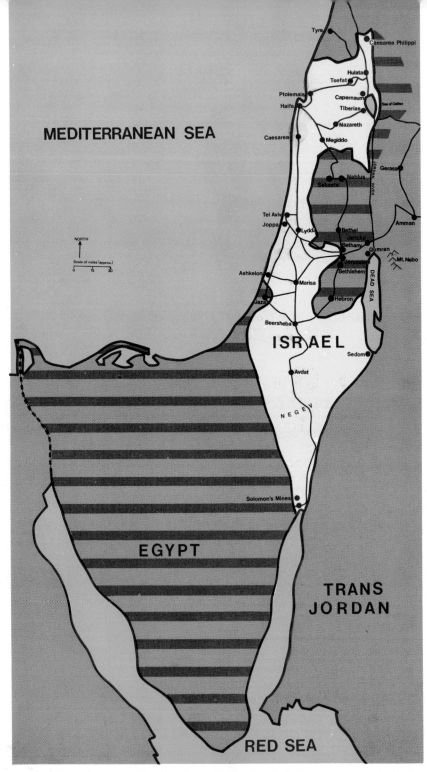

Israel today showing the border which divided the country after the 1948 war and the area (striped) obtained by Israel during the 1967 six-day war.

PALESTINE, the country which has become known as the Holy Land or Bible Land, is a rugged, arid, small area bordering on the eastern shores of the Mediterranean Sea. So far as is yet known, the country contains only scanty mineral wealth, no important oil deposits, and with the exception of a few isolated areas, this rocky land is even hostile to agriculture.

Yet, down through the ages, no other spot on the face of the globe has played such an important role in the history of civilization. No other area has been so frequently and violently fought over as this small strip of land whose total area covers only approximately 12,000 square miles.

The answer to Palestine's historic importance can only be found in geography and religion. Geographically, over the centuries, the little country of Palestine straddled the important land trade routes from the agriculturally rich Euphrates-Tigris valleys to the militarily and culturally important lands of Egypt. During the long period when these two civilizations contended with each other, their armies by physical necessity traveled back and forth over the narrow strip of Mediterranean coast land which is known as Palestine and there met in violent combat so many times that history virtually has lost the count.

A more accurate and adequate answer to the puzzle of Palestine's importance can be found, however, in this little country's tremendous religious significance. Three of the world's great religions

claim this area as their birthplaces and as the prime region of their development. Here, in the hills and valleys of this rugged country, Judaism had its birth. The Moslems, whose Islamic faith was founded by Mohammed, claim their ancestry through Abraham, who was the first great prophet to settle in this area. This also was the land of Jesus of Nazareth. His Christian ideals and principles were taught and dramatized here largely in the 85-mile area between Galilee and the Judean hills.

For the many millions of members of these three great religions, Palestine is a holy land. Most of the many wars that have been fought here have been motivated out of religious controversy or fervor. The majority of the historical places that can be visited in this area are either religious shrines or are closely connected with events that transpired in religious history.

Abraham and the Promised Land

The recorded history of the Bible Land began with a pilgrimage of a Hebrew named Abraham. Little is known of the ancestry of Abraham, who, on instructions of the Lord, left his people and his home in the land of the Chaldees, apparently near what is now Basra in Iraq, and traveled north and west toward a promised land. Abraham was a Semite whose ancestors had probably come from the Arabian peninsula and had settled among the Sumerians in the valleys between the two great

rivers, the Euphrates and the Tigris. Intermarrying with the non-Semitic Sumerians, his progenitors probably later became known as the Babylonians, Chaldeans, and Assyrians.

Abraham's father seems to have been a manufacturer and dealer in idols. Abraham soon lost confidence in these man-made gods. Seeking a more acceptable Creator, Abraham received his inspiration and guidance, and taking a small group of his immediate family with him, set out for a promised land away from the idolatrous influence of his homeland.

The party traveled northwest toward Haran where they sojourned for a season and where Abraham's father, Terah, died. In all likelihood, Abraham and his party knew where they were going on this first leg of their journey. Haran was the land of a Semitic people known as the Amorites. The fact that these people were friendly and welcomed the "strangers" and also in view of the fact that the city was named Haran, the name of Abraham's brother—the father of his nephew, Lot—would seem to indicate that the Amorites, if not actual relatives, were close acquaintances of Abraham and his people.

After a short stay in Haran, Abraham took his wife, his nephew Lot, and "the souls that they had gotten in Haran" and went west and south into the strange land of Canaan. Apparently, Abraham taught the Amorites about Jehovah, the all-power-

5

ful God he had discovered, and had converted some of them to this concept. It would seem that, "the souls that they had gotten in Haran" (Gen. 12:5) were actually converts who had accepted Abraham's new, dynamic religion.

The land of Canaan was already inhabited by a people known as the Canaanites. They had established a number of communities and fortified areas in the country through which Abraham traveled.

Abraham's first stop was at Shechem, where he built an altar and gave thanks unto his God. The party then moved on south to Bethel, where another altar was constructed. Then, "there was a famine in the land; and Abraham went down into Egypt" obviously to obtain food and supplies.

After a sojourn in Egypt, the party returned to Bethel and then moved on south and made permanent residence in the Plains of Mamra, at Hebron.

Abraham's Posterity

In the Plains of Mamra, two sons were born to Abraham. Ishmael, the firstborn, was the son of Hagar, Abraham's wife Sarah's, handmaiden. Ishmael became a hunter and a man of the desert and is believed to be the ancestor of the Arabs.

In their old ages, a second son, Isaac, was born to Abraham and Sarah. Isaac was a preferred son, and through him the Lord's blessing and covenant were perpetuated. Abraham sent back to Haran, from among his own people, for a wife for his son Isaac and from her Isaac had twin sons, Esau and Jacob. Esau, the firstborn, later sold his birthright to Jacob, and the covenant Abraham made with his god was continued through Jacob.

Isaac and his son Jacob were capable agriculturalists and they prospered and multiplied extensively in the land of Canaan. Jacob, whose name had been changed to Israel, had twelve sons and from them the Twelve Tribes of Israel descended.

One of these sons, Joseph, was Jacob's favorite and because his love for him created jealousy among Joseph's brothers, they sold him to a caravan which carried him into Egypt. There Joseph prospered and eventually became second only to Pharaoh as a ruler in Egypt.

Joseph's great wisdom and his programs of conservation were great blessings to the Egyptians. But, after many generations, Pharaohs arose who did not remember Joseph and the blessings he had brought them. The Children of Israel, by now numbering approximately 6,000 souls, were put into slavery and bondage and forced under heavy burden to construct Egyptian cities and monuments to Egyptian gods.

The Children of Israel in Egypt

Eventually, due to another famine in Canaan, Jacob brought his family down into Egypt and there, reunited with his son Joseph, the Israelites pros-

7

pered exceedingly, "and the land was filled with them." (Exod. 1:7.)

Moses and the Great Exodus

It was under these circumstances that the great leader Moses arose, reunited the people and, about 1400 years before Christ (there is disagreement as to the exact date), led them away from their captors and oppressors in Egypt back toward the Promised Land.

Under the leadership and prodding of Moses, the people made their successful escape and, after some 40 years of waiting and wandering in the wilderness of Sinai (until a generation which had not known the flesh-pots of Egypt had arisen), Moses and his people reached the mountains of Moab. From here they could look down into the oasis of Jericho and into the Promised Land, a land, however, which Moses himself was forbidden to enter.

Joshua and the Conquest of the Promised Land

After Moses' death, Joshua led the Children of Israel in a successful conquest of the country and established them with reasonable security in their Promised Land. After Joshua's death, however, no leader arose who was strong enough to hold the tribes together. There followed a long period of inner strife and dissensions. During these times the tribes were preserved and kept intact only through the efforts of a series of wise and usually good men who served as their judges.

Samuel, Saul, and David

The last of these great judges, or prophets, was Samuel who, before he died, was persuaded by the people to appoint a king. Samuel reluctantly anointed Saul king. But when, as he expected, Saul disappointed him, Samuel secretly anointed a young harpist, David, as king.

Then followed a period of bitter conflict between Saul and David until, after Saul's death, David became king of all Israel.

David was a mighty general and leader. He unified and strengthened the people, conquered Jerusalem, which until then had remained in the hands of the Jebusites, and pushed out the boundaries of the land to their greatest extent in history. Israel became a powerful and important country.

After the glory of the Davidic period, the reins of the kingdom passed from David into the hands of his son, Solomon. Solomon inherited the kingdom at the height of its geographical scope and power.

Disintegration and Dispersion[1]

Unlike his father, Solomon did not add to Israel's holdings, but rather concentrated on its economic and cultural development. He improved trade and built great cities and completed construction of the

----

[1]Some of the material for this section is from "The Scattering of Israel," by O. Preston Robinson, *The Instructor*, August 1960, p. 264. Used by permission of the editors.

beautiful temple at Jerusalem. To support his expanded economic program, Solomon divided the land into tax districts so that the growing tax burden could be more easily administered. This administrative division conformed roughly to the geographical areas already divided among the Twelve Tribes and hence set the stage for the tribal division and conflicts which later brought about the people's destruction.

Kingdom Split into Judah and Israel

After Solomon's death, the kingdom which had been united by David was again split, this time into two parts. Judah, comprising the tribes of Judah, Simeon, and Benjamin, established itself in the south with Jerusalem as headquarters. Israel, consisting of the remaining tribes, was in the north centered at Samaria. This was the period, roughly 900 B.C., of the severe struggles between Solomon's son Rehoboam, king of Judah, and Jeroboam, the young Ephraimite officer to whom Solomon had entrusted such great power and confidence. The wars between these two leaders and their peoples divided and weakened the kingdoms and opened the way for their conquest by outsiders.

It was during this period (approximately 875-850 B.C.) that the prophets Elijah and Elisha pleaded with the people to repent and warned them that if they continued in their unrighteousness they would be severely persecuted and scattered. It was also during this period that Samaria was besieged and the first reference was made to the possible scattering of some of the Children of Israel.

The split of Israel into the two fragments of Israel and Judah and the resulting wars and conflicts between the two houses opened the door for invasions from outsiders. During this period, the Egyptians campaigned successfully against Judah and, according to secular history, also captured many towns and cities in Israel. It is quite likely that these invaders, in addition to the material plunder of war, carried many Israelite slaves back into their country.

Also, a bit later, during the reign of Ahab, Samaria was besieged and, although the invaders were defeated, scriptural evidence is provided that many Israelites had been transplanted into the territory around Damascus. (1 Kings 20:34.)

The first extensive dispersion of Israel, however, took place during the reign of the Assyrian king, Tiglath-pileser III. In approximately 734 B.C., after subjugating the eastern cities, this king turned his attention to the west, took Damascus, and then placed the whole of Israel under his control. In the process of this conquest, Tiglath-pileser took a large number of Israelite leaders captive into Assyria.

The Fall of Samaria

Samaria, however, successfully resisted this invasion but Tiglath-pileser's successor, Shalmaneser, laid siege to the city. Samaria held out for another three years, but Shalmaneser's successor, Sargon II, overpowered the fortress and led 27,290 prominent Israelites as captives back into Babylonia. In an effort once and for all to stamp out the Israelite kingdom, Sargon replaced these people with strangers from the cities of Babylon and the Medes. This was the beginning of the Samaritans, the strangers in the land so despised by the Jews at the time of Jesus. It was during this period that the prophets Amos and Hosea, and later Isaiah, preached to the people and tried, without permanent success, to persuade them to desist from their evil ways.

The fall of Samaria left Judah still independent but uneasy and insecure. Because Uzziah continued to pay tribute to the Assyrians, Judah was left virtually undisturbed until after Sargon's death. In 701, however, a revolt occurred and the new Assyrian king, Sennacherib, invaded Judah, captured many of the smaller towns, and invested Jerusalem. It was at this time that Isaiah came forth and declared Jerusalem to be the City of God and inviolable. This saved Jerusalem from destruction, but many Jews were carried off into captivity. It was apparently during this period also that colonies of Jews were established in Egypt. (Jeremiah 44:10.)

The Babylonian Conquests

Jerusalem and the surrounding territory now were in a precarious position. The people were slipping deeper and deeper into iniquity, and the great teacher, Jeremiah, was uttering his prophetic predictions regarding the ultimate destruction of the city. During this period many groups left Jerusalem, including Lehi and his family.

A new military power was rising in the east. The Assyrian kingdom was tottering, and Babylonia's dynamic leader, Nebuchadnezzar, was on the march. In the west the Egyptians were rising in strength, and in 608 B.C. Necho led an Egyptian army into Palestine which carried more Jews into captivity.

Jerusalem wavered between obedience to Babylon or alliance with Egypt and mistakenly chose the latter. The angered Nebuchadnezzar marched on the city and completely destroyed it and most of Palestine in two separate attacks in 598 and 586 B.C.

Cyrus the Persian

Despite its military victories, the Babylonian Empire, characteristic of all who conquer by the sword, was disintegrating from within and, in line with history's ever-moving pace, a new power was ready to step in to take control. In 539 B.C., Cyrus the Great of Persia completed his conquest of Babylon and took with his plunder what was left of the vassal states of Israel and Judah.

The Persian rule, however, was a benevolent one. Cyrus reversed the Syrian and Babylonian policies of deportation of the Israelites and instituted a program of the restoration of captive peoples to their former homes. Thus was begun the reconstruction of the Hebrew state which continued under the rules of Darius I and Artaxerxes I. During this period the reconstruction at the temple at Jerusalem was completed in 516 B.C. Also, led by the prophets Ezra and Nehemiah respectively, additional bands of Israelites returned to their homeland and began building Hebrew religious life back to its original status. It was during this period that Ezra completed the compilation and editing of the first five books now in the Old Testament (the Pentateuch) and laid the groundwork for the reorganization of Jewish life in accordance with the Mosaic laws. From the work of Ezra and Nehemiah and with the watchful approval of the Persian rulers, the Hebrew kingdom grew eventually to approximately half the size it enjoyed before it was destroyed 125 years earlier by the Babylonians.

During this Persian period many Hebrews prospered and became influential in eastern cities. A substantial number of these never did return to Palestine. Their descendants formed the nucleus of the community of Jews which flourished in Iraq until 1948, when the violent Arab-Israeli conflicts motivated their return to the new state of Israel.

Alexander Takes Over

Again, history repeated itself. The Persian empire began to crumble from within and from the military pressures of the Greek, Alexander the Great. In 331 B.C. Alexander conquered the area of Palestine and incorporated it into the Greek Empire. His reign, however, was relatively short-lived. When he died in 323 B.C. his two chief generals, Seleucus Nicator and Ptolemy, fought over and divided the kingdom.

The Seleucids established their headquarters in Syria and Phoenicia. The Ptolemies were centered in Egypt and Alexandria. Palestine lay in between, and the two warring nations never ceased fighting over it. During the next 25 years Jerusalem changed hands seven times, and over the years Palestine was won and lost so many times that even an estimated count is impossible. During this troubled period thousands of Hebrews were either taken into captivity or left voluntarily to settle in the north or in the south. The historian Philo estimated that in A.D. 38-41 there were more than a million Jews in Egypt. Thousands of others migrated or were driven to Antioch and to the cities of the north and from there spread out to Media, Persia, Armenia and farther to the east and north.

The Maccabaean Restoration

A second period of restoration took place, however, during the reign of the Maccabaeans. In 168 B.C., Mattathias, a Hebrew priest, refused to worship at the Altar of Zeus which had been erected by Antiochus throughout the land. In the ensuing struggle, Mattathias killed a Greek soldier and then took his family and fled into the hills. Many other Jewish families soon joined him and a full-scale

15

revolt developed. Judas Maccabaeus, one of Mattathias' sons, organized a series of guerilla attacks on the Greeks and their garrisons which later resulted in the recapture of much of Palestine and restored Jewish worship to the temple in Jerusalem. A subsequent Maccabaean warrior, Alexander Jannaeus, eventually reconquered all of Palestine and reestablished the Hebrew state.

These happy circumstances, however, were not to last for long. During this period a new division arose among the Jews. The Pharisees, who favored ritual purity, quarreled and fought with the Sadducees, who favored a more worldly approach to religious affairs. After the death of Jannaeus, his two sons, Hyrcanus II (pro-Pharisee) and Aristobulus II (pro-Sadducee) fought over the kingdom and both made the mistake, unknown to each other, of appealing to the Roman Pompey for help. Pompey prudently bided his time. When both sides were so weakened as to offer only feeble resistance, in 63 B.C. he moved in, captured Jerusalem, and took over all of Palestine. This was the beginning of the Roman domination and the end of Jewish independence until the recent establishment, on May 14, 1948, of the new state of Israel.

The Long Roman Domination

During the Roman period, both under Pompey and later under Julius Caesar, the administrative power over Palestine was given to Antipater, the Idumean. During his administration a number of

Jewish revolts were crushed, and for his efforts Antipater was made a citizen of Rome. His son Phasel was made governor of Jerusalem and his other son, Herod, governor of Galilee.

Due to his devotion to the emperor, in 40 B.C., under Mark Anthony, Herod was appointed king of Judah. After his death, his kingdom was divided among three of his sons. Later, in A.D. 6, Herod's descendants were deposed by Emperor Augustus. From A.D. 6 to A.D. 40, Judea was ruled by Roman procurators, the most famous of whom was Pontius Pilate. During most of this time the Romans left the Jews free to worship much as they pleased.

The Romans were primarily interested in taxes, a burden which they imposed heavily upon the people. Due to this heavy load and also because some of the procurators were ruthless in their administrations, the Jews rose in revolt many times. During one of these, between A.D. 66 and A.D. 70, a state of warfare existed between Rome and Jerusalem and, finally, the Roman general Titus, son of Vespasian, attacked Jerusalem. After five months he completely destroyed the city and the temple and carried away its religious objects and treasury. This was the final destruction of the temple. Jerusalem, however, was later rebuilt by the Romans after they had crushed a rebellion by Simon bar Kochba. They renamed the city Aelia Capitolina, and the Jews were forbidden to enter it. This was in A.D. 132.

The Arab Conquests

For a period of several hundred years the Jews remained under the subjugation of the Romans. Then in approximately A.D. 610, a new religion, started by an Arab named Mohammed, grew rapidly and spread across the face of this area. After Mohammed's death, the Moslems pushed his doctrines forward and in a series of holy wars conquered all of the Middle East, North Africa, and across the Straits of Gibraltar to all of Spain. Jerusalem fell to the Moslems in A.D. 638.

Typical of conquering invaders, division broke out among the Moslems. For a period of several hundred years Palestine moved from the control of one group to another, the people never quite knowing who their conquerors were. In A.D. 877 the country was won by a Turkish colony out of Egypt. It changed hands several times and then, finally, was conquered again by the Fatimids of Egypt.

Then followed the conquests of the crusaders whose holy wars desecrated the area for some 200 years.

After the crusaders Palestine fell under the rule of the Ottoman Turks, who also quarreled among themselves, but managed to hold on to the territory until the British took it over during World War I.

Zionism vs. Arab Nationalism

As the Turkish empire began to disintegrate, the

seeds of Arab nationalism began to sprout. After centuries of subjugation from outside sources, the Arab peoples once again sensed the possibilities of unity and self-determination.

Unfortunately, these seeds of nationalism germinated at approximately the same time that Jewish Zionism began to take root. With the pograms in Russia and the violent anti-Hebrew sentiment in many Eastern European countries, persecution of the Jews had again begun to rise. These persecutions and fears re-ignited the flame of desire among the Jewish people to find a permanent home of their own.

As early as 1860, encouraged by an imaginative book by Theodore Herzl entitled *The Jewish State,* substantial groups of Jews all over the world again began to dream of a national home in Palestine. Many of these people immigrated to their ancient "home" and at first they were welcomed by Arab residents who sold them land and helped them to get established in their new area.

This friendship, however, was not to last. As larger numbers came into Palestine, the "yishuv," or Jewish community, was established in growing numbers, and concern and fear developed among the Arabs that if the Jews were not stopped, they would eventually dominate. Over the years, this apprehension grew in intensity, with numerous incidents which were motivated and reacted to by both sides. In 1917, the British Balfour Declaration was incorporated into the League of Nations Mandates. This declaration stated "that his Majesty's Government view with favor the establishment in Palestine of a national home for the Jewish people." The stage was now fully set for serious conflict between these two peoples whose ancestral ties came from the same source.

During World War I, the Turks were allied with the Germans. The British, with their French allies, reasoned that if they could motivate the Arabs to rise up in revolt against their Turkish masters, a second front could be established which would divert German arms from Central Europe. Consequently, British generals Allenby and Lawrence made contact with Arab chieftains and promised them that if they would rally armies and attack the Turks, their dream of nationalism, supported by the British, could be realized. The Arab chieftains accepted this promise and, together with British assistance, were successful in routing the Turks. The Arab-British armies marched victoriously into Damascus.

However, possibly unknown to the British generals and certainly as a surprise to the Arab leaders, the British and the French, in 1916, entered into the secret Sykes-Picot Agreement under which the two major powers agreed to divide up the territory between themselves. This agreement later was translated into the League of Nations Mandate under which Britain was given control of Palestine, Trans-Jordan, and Iraq. France was granted control over

Lebanon and Syria. This agreement, which the Arabs considered as a vicious doublecross, plus the Balfour Declaration, motivated the violence which later erupted into the 1948 Arab-Israeli conflict.

The 1948 Arab-Israeli War

After the Balfour Declaration, Jewish immigration into Palestine multiplied enormously. Violent conflicts and incidents grew in momentum until the British decided to withdraw their mandates over the area. This occurred in 1947 and led immediately to the outbreak of the bitterly fought 1948 Arab-Israeli conflict. This conflict, a full-scale war, was stopped by the United Nations, which established a tenuous and hostile border between the two peoples. This unnatural border snaked up through the center of Jerusalem and through the middle of the land, disecting it in half and serving as a buffer zone between deep hatreds and animosities on both sides.

Following the cessation of hostilities, the Jewish people declared the formation of the new State of Israel, which, with the exception of the disillusioned Arab nations, was soon recognized by the great powers around the world.

The unrealistic division set up by the United Nations persisted for 20 years. Yet, the country maintained a tenuous peace but interrupted by many border incidents and by a brief conflict, in 1956, over the Suez Canal.

Nevertheless, all of the problems faced by the two peoples still persisted and their solutions became even more difficult. Thousands of Arab refugees either had been driven out of their homeland or had left in the face of war's threat. There remained festering hatred over territories taken by force or granted by edict. There was the Suez Canal, now closed to Israeli traffic. To the Israeli there was the threat of Arab domination of the Straits of Biran and the closing of this sea access to Israeli exports and imports.

The 1967 Six-Day War

All of these, plus a rising military strength in certain of the Arab countries, supported by Russia, together with mounting threats of armed conflict on both sides, finally led to the violent six-day war which erupted during the early days of June, 1967. In this war, although outnumbered some 20 to one, the Jews achieved a stunning victory which moved their borders back to the natural barrier of the Jordan River. The Israelis also took a section above the Sea of Galilee known as the Golan Heights and, in order to protect their sea lanes from and through the Red Sea, overran the entire Sinai Peninsula.

This war, although a great victory for the Jews, still has not settled the basic problems which exist and which demand solution in the area. These remain to be studied and resolved and it seems obvious that only mutually agreed-upon political solutions will prove to be practical.

Israel's Bible Lands

The ancient biblical sites and the sacred shrines

scattered so widely over this area are now largely under Israeli control. These fantastic, sacred places are of deep religious significance to people of all faiths all over the world, and despite the turbulence and uncertainties that still exist in the area, they are of great historical attraction.

Since the six-day war and the enlargement of the sovereign state of Israel, archaeological exploration of biblical sites has been accelerated and much evidence is being uncovered which confirms the accuracy of the Bible. In fact, the Bible, along with Flavius Josephus' dramatic histories, is being used to guide the archaeologists in some of their explorations. Through these, proof is being gathered that many of the spectacular events described in the Bible did take place in the areas as described. The walls of Jericho, for example, did fall basically as Joshua said they did. The Bible has been used to help find Solomon's Mines, to fix the actual places where important historical, biblical battles were fought, and even to help present-day farmers decide what trees and crops will grow in the area most successfully.

As one walks through the past in this fabulous country, either by reading about these great historical events or through personal visits, the Bible again comes to life. One can walk and, mentally, enjoy the stimulating association of such great prophets as Abraham, Moses, Elijah, Isaiah, Jeremiah, and Ezekial and can be motivated by the simple lives and teachings of Jesus of Nazareth and of his dis-

23

ciples, Peter, James, John, Matthew, Luke, and Paul. Through the explorations of what has been accomplished and is still going on, the great traditions and inspiration of these remarkable ancient times combine to motivate a more extensive and deeper application of the divine principles of living exemplified in the lives and teachings of these great religious leaders.

References:

1. *The Dictionary of the Bible,* ed., James Hastings (New York: Scribners, 1952).
2. Talmage, James E., *The Articles of Faith* (Salt Lake City: The Church of Jesus Christ of Latter-day Saints, 1949).
3. Charles, R. H., "The Apocalypse of Baruch," "I and II Maccabees," "The Letter of Aristeas," *The Pseudepigrapha of the Old Testament* (New York: Oxford Press, 1913).
4. Ellis, Harvey B., *Israel and the Middle East* (New York: Ronald Press, 1957).
5. Learsi, Rufus, *Israel—A History of the Jewish People* (Cleveland: World Publishing Company, 1949).
6. Mould, Elmer, *Essentials of Bible History* (New York: Ronald Press, 1951).
7. American Friends Service Committee, *Search for Peace in the Middle East* (Philadelphia, 1970).
8. Dimont, Max I., *Jews, God and History* (New York: Simon and Schuster, 1962).
9. Josephus, Flavius, *The Antiquities of the Jews, The Wars of the Jews* (various translations and editions).

Army tank captured in the Golan Heights.

Jerusalem

city of uneasy peace

A general view of the city of Jerusalem as it looks today.

"*Pray for the peace of Jerusalem:
they shall prosper that love thee.
Peace be within thy walls, and
prosperity within thy palaces.*"
(Psalm 122:6-7.)

A general view of the Jerusalem area, with the Mount of Olives in the
center background.

JERUSALEM is a city of contrasts and contradictions. Although since antiquity probably the most fought-over place in the world, Jerusalem, physically and economically, has never been any great military prize.

Located on the crest of the Judean hills, Jerusalem is not a part of any important trade route. It controls no seaport or coast. No rivers flow near it. Its terrain is rugged, rocky, and extremely hostile to agriculture. Even its water supply is scanty and inadequate. The only native spring is deep under one of the city's four hills and flows only intermittently into one of the deep ravines or valleys.

For the survival of the city and its inhabitants, water must be brought through aqueducts from surrounding areas. Moreover, with the exception of a relatively few short periods, Jerusalem's walls have never contained any great treasures.

Yet, despite all these inadequacies, Jerusalem has always been a choice prize for conquerors. Since recorded times, the city has been sieged, defended and conquered so many times that even the number has been lost in confusion.

Successively, Jerusalem has been held and lost by the Canaanites, the Jebusites, the Israelites, Jews, Greeks, Romans, Arabs, Crusaders, Turks, and the British. The most recent battle over the city was the violently fought 1967 war between the Arabs and the Jews, the effects of which are still discernible on some of Jerusalem's streets and in many of the city's buildings.

Today, as throughout its eventful and tragic history, Jerusalem, although under Israel control, is still a city of uncertain future.

The name Jerusalem, literally translated, means "possession of peace," "City of Peace," or the "Holy City." Yet, although the city still carries the name "peace," down through the ages, Jerusalem has experienced little tranquillity. Shortly before his crucifixion, Jesus of Nazareth pondered the condition and fate of the city and lamented, "O Jerusalem, Jerusalem, thou that killest the prophets, and stonest them which are sent unto thee, how often would I have gathered thy children together, even as a hen gathereth her chickens under her wings, and ye would not!" (Matt. 23:37.)

The origin of the founding of Jerusalem is lost in the obscurity of antiquity. Possibly the first reference to the city was made approximately 2000 B.C. when, as recorded in Genesis, Abraham met and was blessed by Melchizedek, King of Salem, and paid tithes to him. (Gen. 14:18-20.) Some scholars believe that Salem, meaning "peace," was the original of the present Jerusalem.

Approximately 1350 B.C. Abid-Heba, King of Urusalim, sent a letter to his Egyptian overlord in which he complained about certain conditions in his city. This letter, referring to Jerusalem, was discovered during the excavations of Tel el-Amarna, Egypt, and is presently included as a part of the correspondence obtained from this archaeological discovery.

In pre-Davidic times, Jerusalem was probably situated on a hill known as Ophel. This is one of the main ridges on which the present city is built, the high point of which is known as Mount Moriah. This hill has played a significantly important role during Jerusalem's long and eventful history.

During the conquest of Palestine, Joshua was unable to subdue Jerusalem. The city apparently remained in the hands of the Jebusites until some 400 years later when it was conquered by King David. David immediately brought the Ark of the Covenant into the city and began elaborate plans to house it there permanently. David made the city his permanent headquarters and from there conducted his many campaigns which stretched Israel's borders to encompass the largest territory in the country's history. David, however, was thwarted in his attempt to build a temple in the city in which to house the Ark of the Covenant. He died and is believed to have been buried on Mount Zion in the city.

David's son Solomon consolidated his father's conquests and employed his great power to build spectacular structures throughout the country, but chiefly at Jerusalem. Here, among other magnificent buildings, he constructed a beautiful temple on the top of Mount Moriah.

During Solomon's reign, Jerusalem must have been a beautiful city, indeed.

After Solomon's time, the city was seized by the

Egyptians and its religious treasures removed. Later it was again pillaged by a coalition of Arabs and Philistines and then by the Israelites themselves who had been separated into the two warring camps of Israel and Judah.

In 587 B.C. the city and Solomon's temple were destroyed by the Babylonian Nebuchadnezzar. Then followed a series of sieges and conquests during which the city and its temple were destroyed several times, culminating in their final destruction and in the dispersion of the Jews in approximately 70 A.D.

During the lifetime of Jesus of Nazareth, Jerusalem was probably again at a peak of its glory. Herod the Great had rebuilt the city on a grand scale and had restored the temple to probably even greater magnificence than it was in Solomon's times. It was under these circumstances, only a few days before his crucifixion, that Jesus paused on the road up the hill near Bethany and looked and beheld the city in all of its splendor, "and wept over it." (Luke 19:41.) In all probability, he wept not only because of leaving the beautiful city, but also because of what it might have been and the peace that it might have enjoyed, had its inhabitants accepted his teachings and those of the prophets.

Undoubtedly, the reason why Jerusalem has been such a historical prize for conquerors lies in its tremendous religious significance. This embattled, insecure, and fought-over city is truly a holy place. Its many religious shrines are closely connected with the origin and development of three of the world's great religions.

The Jews claim Jerusalem as their holy city, the City of David, the City of Solomon. Here on the top of Mount Moriah, according to the Old Testament, Abraham brought his son Isaac to offer him in sacrifice as commanded by the Lord. Here David lived, reigned, and triumphed. Here Solomon built his beautiful edifices. Countless Hebrew prophets and kings flourished, lived, and died in this great city.

For the Moslems, along with Mecca and Medina, Jerusalem is a holy place. It is a city of deep religious tradition. From the top of Mount Moriah, Moslems believe that Mohammed ascended to heaven. Here, one of their great mosques, the Mosque of Omar, also known as the Dome of the Rock, was constructed. Although destroyed, this great mosque has been rebuilt. Today it is a holy place which all orthodox Moslems should visit at least once during their lifetimes.

For the Christians, Jerusalem was the place where Jesus accomplished much of his mighty work. Here he gave many of his great teachings and performed many of his most wonderful miracles. It was here that mothers brought to him their little children "and he took them in his arms, put his hands upon them, and blessed them." (Mark 10:16.)

In Jerusalem, Jesus healed the sick, caused the lame to walk, and made the blind to see. Here,

33

also, he exhibited his righteous indignation when he cast the thieves and money changers out of the temple and proclaimed that his Father's house "shall be called the house of prayer; but ye have made it a den of thieves." (Matt. 21:13.)

Under the stately olive trees in the Garden of Gethsemane, his "soul exceedingly sorrowful, even unto death," Jesus prayed unto his Father, saying, "O my Father, if it be possible, let this cup pass from me. Nevertheless, not as I will, but as thou wilt." (Matt. 26:38, 39.)

It was on a Jerusalem hill now known as the Mount of Evil Counsel that Caiaphas conspired to have Jesus condemned. It was up the winding streets of this old city that he carried his cross to Calvary (Golgotha), where he was crucified. It was here, in the beautiful garden of Joseph of Arimathea, that his body was laid and that the glorious events of the resurrection took place. It was on the slopes of the Mount of Olives, near Bethany, that Jesus ascended to heaven and that he gave his final instructions to his followers to preach his gospel to all the world, "baptizing them in the name of the Father, and of the Son, and of the Holy Ghost."

Even in its present uncertain and embattled condition, Jerusalem is still a holy and sacred place. Its many religious shrines are visited by countless thousands of emigrants from all religious faiths.

The Mosque of Omar—also known as the Dome of the Rock, built on Mount Moriah over the spot where it is believed Abraham prepared to offer his son Isaac in sacrifice.

Jerusalem

shrines and dramatic antiquities

The Garden of Gethsemane with the Church of the Nations in the center.

"Then cometh Jesus with them
unto a place called Gethsemane,
and saith unto the disciples, Sit
ye here, while I go and pray
yonder." (Matt. 26:36.)

*A **hill outside** of the walls of Jerusalem believed by some to be Golgotha, the place of the crucifixion.*

SOMEONE has observed that if one happened to stub his toe in the Bible Land he quite likely would kick out an important artifact connected with the rich history of this ancient country, Israel. If this could be true in respect to the entire country of Israel, it is even more descriptive of Jerusalem itself. Almost every square foot of this historic city is deeply etched with the imprint of history.

The four hills and the three valleys where Jerusalem is situated are all extensively imbedded with archaeological evidences of the long, eventful history of this ancient city. Scattered all over this confined area are shrines, sacred places, and some spots of unfortunate evil notoriety connected with significant events that have occurred here over the past 4,000 years.

To describe all of the shrines and sacred places that can be visited in Jerusalem would require much more space than is available in this short chapter. The following are a few of the more important places which, each year, are visited by thousands of interested people from all religious faiths and from most countries of the world.

The Mount of Olives

Although not considered one of Jerusalem's hills because it was never included in the walled city, the Mount of Olives to Christians is one of Jerusalem's most sacred areas. At the foot of this impressive hill, located in rugged territory, is the little town of *Bethany*, where Jesus spent many of his evenings when he was in the Jerusalem area. Bethany is where the home of Mary, Martha, and Lazarus was located.

It will be recalled that Lazarus was sick and the sisters hurriedly sent word to Jesus to come and administer to him. Jesus was delayed and before he arrived, Lazarus died. Then occurred the marvelous miracle of Lazarus' being raised from the dead.

In Bethany, one can visit the street which is believed to have been where Mary, Martha, and Lazarus lived. Also, a tomb there is pointed out as being the one where Lazarus' body laid.

Near the bottom of the Mount of Olives is the Garden of Gethsemane with the beautiful Church of the Nations at its entrance. Inside the garden are the twisted, old olive trees which may have been there when Jesus knelt and prayed to his father. A little farther up the hill is the site where the village of Bethpage was once located. It was from here that Jesus obtained the donkey on which he rode during his last triumphal entry into Jerusalem.

On the top of the hill is an edifice which marks the spot where some believe the resurrected Christ's ascension took place. Although it is more likely that the ascension occurred farther down the hill near Bethany, all of this ground experienced sacred events.

40

The four hills, or ridges, around and on which

the walled city of Jerusalem is situated are known as Zion, Ophel, Acra, and Bezetha. Each of these has shared importantly in the city's history, particularly in its many sieges, defenses, and conquests. It was on the points of these hills that King Uzziah built some of his extensive fortifications which made the city so impregnable during his reign.

Mount Zion is where Jesus attended the last supper before his crucifixion. It also is believed to be where David's tomb rests and, possibly, is also the burial place of Mary, the mother of Jesus.

These three shrines are all located near the summit of Mount Zion and are adjacent to an important Moslem Mosque. The room which is believed to be the one in which the Last Supper was held, is, in all probability, not authentic. Considerable debris has accumulated over the centuries and most authorities believe that the actual room must have been several feet below the present surface of the ground.

As with most of the shrines and holy places in Jerusalem, their actual locations are hotly contested. The visitor's greatest satisfaction comes from the knowledge that he is within close proximity of where these great events took place.

Mount Ophel, another of Jerusalem's main ridges, rises through the heart of the old city. The upper part of this hill, known as Mount Moriah, is believed to be where Abraham, as commanded by the Lord, brought his son Isaac for a sacrifice.

Solomon's temple was built on Mount Moriah

41

and, according to a Moslem legend, it was from a rock on this hill that Mohammed ascended to heaven. The Mosque of Omar was built over this site. Later this mosque was destroyed, and the present one, also known as the Dome of the Rock, was constructed here.

Near the western entrance to the temple area on Mount Moriah, a portion of the wall that once surrounded Solomon's temple court is partially exposed. This is the famous *wailing wall* which, although nearly destroyed, is one of the holy Jewish sites. It is believed that the lowest part of this wall actually dates from the time of Solomon's temple.

Rising up out of the heart of the lower city is *Mount Acra,* another of Jerusalem's hills. This hill, too, is rich in the history of ancient Jerusalem. Presently, its chief shrine attraction is the *Via Dolorosa* which winds through the lower city, up this ridge, and out the walls to where Golgotha is believed to have been located. It was up this narrow, winding Street of Sorrows on the way to the crucifixion that it is believed Jesus carried his cross and that he stumbled and fell and Simon from Cyrene picked up the cross and carried it for him.

Golgotha is believed by many to have been outside the walls of the city. Presently, two separate sites have been selected but no proof exists as to whether either is the exact spot. The Church of the Holy Sepulchre is claimed to have been built on one of these sites. Some years ago, however, a

42

tomb was discovered and an old wine press exca-vated in what is now known as the "Garden Tomb." Some believe that this was the Garden of Joseph of Arimathea and that Jesus was buried here. A hill adjacent to the garden, shaped somewhat like a skull, is believed by these authorities to be Golgotha, the actual place where the crucifixion occurred.

Another ridge outside of the old walls is known as the *Mount of Evil Counsel*. Some believe that Caiaphas had a summer house here and it was here that Judas came and made his evil bargain which led to Jesus' condemnation and crucifixion.

The valleys between Jerusalem's hills have also played their significant part in the city's history. Between the Mount of Olives and the old walled city is a valley known as *Kidron*. Jesus walked or rode through this valley many times. It was through this valley that he and his followers walked on the way to Mount Zion and the Last Supper. He came back through the Kidron Valley on his way to the Garden of Gethsemane.

Through this valley, also, came Judas and his motley crowd of priests and the riffraff of the people for the kiss of deception. Then followed the sorrow-ful trek back through the valley and up to the place where Pontius Pilate was staying and where Jesus was tried and condemned. In the Valley of Kidron, also, one can visit the tombs of Zechariah, Absalom, the son of David, and the Apostle James. All of these met violent deaths and are believed to have been buried here.

Several small pools exist in and around Jerusalem. Two of these, the *Pool of Bethesda* and *Siloam,* have important religious significance. It was at Bethesda that Jesus met the cripple who had been trying so long to get into the pool and be healed. Jesus asked him, "Wilt thou be made whole?" When the cripple told him of his problem of getting into the pool, Jesus said, "Take up your bed and walk," and he was healed. (John 5:2-8.)

Today, the Pool of Bethesda is approximately 18 feet below the surface of the ground. This possibly indicates the extent to which rubble and debris, over the centuries, has been piled in on top of some of these old shrines.

The *Pool of Siloam* is mentioned in the Old Testament and is connected with many Old Testament prophets. It is also remembered as the place where Jesus healed the man who had been blind since birth. His disciples wondered if the man's affliction was due to his or his ancestors' sins. Jesus assured them that this was not so. Then, anointing the blind man's eyes, he told him to go wash in the Pool of Siloam. He did and was immediately healed. (John 9:1-7.)

These are only a few of the more important shrines and places scattered throughout the Jerusalem area. Certainly, no area in the world is so rich in religious history and no city has played such an important part in the origin and development of the Hebrew, Moslem, and Christian religions.

The tomb in a garden in Jerusalem believed by some to be the place where Jesus was laid.

Excavations at the Temple Mount

The stunning victory for the Jews in their six-day war with the Arabs in 1967 has proved to be more than just a remarkable military accomplishment. In addition to capturing strategic territories, including the formerly divided city of Jerusalem, the Israelis obtained priceless ancient records and also opened the door for themselves for archaeological excavations at biblical sites not previously available to them.

In the midst of the fighting, one day after the battle of Jerusalem was over, Dr. Yigael Yadin, professor of archaeology and former chief of staff of the Israeli army, obtained from the Jordanians an important untranslated scroll recently discovered near the Dead Sea.

Dr. Yadin immediately began unrolling and translating this scroll, which he says promises to be one of the most important ancient records ever to be discovered. Approximately 28 feet in length, it is the longest scroll yet to come to light.

As his translation progressed Dr. Yadin found that nearly half of the length of the scroll dealt with a description of Solomon's Temple and with certain religious rites performed therein. Consequently, he called this record "The Temple Scroll."

Although Dr. Yadin has yet to publish the final report on his findings, the information so far translated covers the physical measurements of the temple together with an enumeration of sacrifices and offerings performed therein.

A second important dividend the Israelis derived out of the six-day war was the opening of the door to additional areas for archaeological exploration. Probably the most important of these dig areas is at the Temple-Mount itself, which previously was under the control of the Jordanians.

Here, since 1968, extensive excavations and research have been going on in an effort to discover the remains not only of Herod's Temple but also of the second temple and of Solomon's Temple and its immediate environs.

Supervising this archaeological work is Dr. Binyamin Mazar, former president of the Hebrew University, and now head of the archaeological team digging at and around the Temple-Mount.

Dr. Mazar and his team of archaeologists are being helped in their exploration by the information contained in the newly obtained "Temple Scroll" but are also being guided chiefly by the descriptions of the temple site contained in the two great works of the historian Flavius Josephus. These detailed descriptions, are contained in Josephus' works, *The Jewish Wars* and *Jewish Antiquities*. They were written early in the Christion era (A.D. 37-100).

However, possibly because of the fact that during the Jewish Wars Josephus defected to the

Roman side, his historical writings, until recently, were largely ignored or were treated as inaccurate by Jewish scholars.

The discovery in 1947 of the Dead Sea Scrolls focused new light on Josephus' works and has proved that he was both a careful and an accurate historian. Consequently, using these documents as guides, the archaeological team is uncovering the details of his vivid description both of the temple and of its immediate surroundings.

The areas now being uncovered are south of the Temple-Mount, along the entire length of its southern wall. The archaeologists are discovering that Herod, when he rebuilt the temple, extended the Temple-Mount area by "filling in and building up the adjacent slopes and valleys on the east and west and enclosing the great level space thus formed within enormous supporting walls."

The current excavations are uncovering a number of significant antiquities. Josephus wrote of Herod's "Royal Stoa." The foundations of this great building are being unearthed. The historian also wrote of the gates on the southern wall.

These are being found—both having been blocked up centuries ago. In addition, the dig is producing ornamental architectural elements, capitals, columns, friezes, panels, fragments of sun dials, geometrical motifs, floral designs, and many other artifacts and motifs, indicating not only the accuracy of Josephus' description but also testifying to first-class planning and construction on Herod's part.

One of the remarkable discoveries is a monumental stairway approximately 210 feet wide, leading up from the street below to the temple area. A second stairway, some 50 feet wide, parallels this enormous structure. Several pools, hewn out of the rock, have been discovered. The archaeologists believe that these must have been designed for the "ritual purification of pilgrims about to enter the Temple-Mount."

Another significant discovery is a network of subterranean tunnels and channels under the buildings which were probably used as water conduits and possibly, also, as means of entry and egress into the temple area and into Herod's palace.

Dr. Mazar has indicated that the excavation has uncovered a great deal of broken pottery and other artifacts from the first temple. Deeper excavations are being planned in an effort to obtain some of the remains of Solomon's structure.

On the upper levels, of course, many Roman and Byzantine remains have been brought to light. Nevertheless, the chief interest lies in attempting to discover, if possible, what might be found from the Solomon period.

This important excavation at the Temple-Mount is now just finishing its fifth year. Dr. Mazar and his team have already established plans for the next five years and are full of anticipation of what their work will uncover.

Sufficient has already been accomplished, however, to establish full confidence that discoveries of even greater significance lie in the future, and plans have already been formulated to present a public exhibit of the findings to date at the New York Metropolitan Museum.

This exhibit, with miniature models, samples of artifacts, films, and other interesting items, will be patterned somewhat after the format of the Dead Sea Scrolls presentation so successfully exhibited at the British Museum, throughout the British Isles, and in certain areas of the United States.

One of the dramatic incidents connected with Jesus' life, when he was teaching in and around Jerusalem, occurred in the temple built by Herod. This incident, as recorded in the 21st chapter of Matthew, describes Jesus' feelings and actions when he entered the temple and observed the abuses that were occurring therein.

"[He] cast out all of them that sold and bought in the temple, and overthrew the tables of the money changers and the seats of them that sold doves. And said unto them, It is written, My house shall be called the house of prayer; but ye have made it a den of thieves."

50   On another occasion, Jesus told his apostles:

"And I will give unto thee the keys of the kingdom of heaven: and whatsoever thou shalt bind on earth shall be bound in heaven; and whatsoever thou shalt loose on earth shall be loosed in heaven."

As surely as the resurrection is a reality and the human soul eternal, so, too, must human love be eternal. If this is so, the Almighty's plan must have included, as indicated by Jesus, both authority and ordinances which would perpetuate both the marriage covenant and the eternalness of the family.

That these are ancient religious concepts is evident from traditions as described in the Old Testament which required that if a husband die, his wife should marry his brother, if he had one, so that seed, or children, could be raised to the deceased brother.

It is doubtful that this tradition would have persisted unless a procedure, or ordinance, existed which would have made it possible for the deceased brother to enjoy his children in the hereafter.

That this tradition, or concept, did exist even down to the time of Christ is apparent from an incident recorded in the 22nd chapter of Matthew and in Mark, 12th chapter. These scriptures record the occasion when the Sadducees attempted to confuse and trap Jesus by asking him about the woman whose husband had died and who, according to the law of Moses, had married, in succession, six of his brothers. They wanted to know which of the brothers would have her as wife in the resurrection.

If a religious ordinance had not existed which, with authority, would make this union possible, it certainly is doubtful that the Sadducees would have referred to this concept which had come down to them from the teachings of Moses.

In commenting on these scriptures, and on the eternalness of the marriage and family concept, Dr. J. R. Dummelow writes: "The pre-Christian book of Enoch says that the righteous after the resurrection shall live so long that they shall beget thousands. This doctrine is also advanced by Rabbi Saadia (who says there will be family relationships in the resurrection). Maimonides also advances this doctrine. He says, 'Men after the resurrection shall use meat and drink and will beget children.'" Further evidence of the eternalness of temple ordinances was recently uncovered in an ancient document which now rests in the British Museum with copies of the same, or a similar one, in several other museums around the world. This document, known as the Testament of Levi, translated by Dr. R. H. Charles, purports to be a record kept by Levi, third son of Jacob.

The document gives a description, written in the first person, of Levi's experiences when he saw the temple in a dream together with certain temple ordinances. This description exists in renditions in many languages, including Armenian, Greek, Slavonic, and Syrica, and may indicate the existence of ancient temple rites. This old description is accepted by the British Museum authorities as having been written in A.D. 874.

Of course, we are not sure what rites, if any, were practiced or what ordinances administered in Solomon's Temple or in any of the less permanent temple-like structures that may have existed before Solomon's time.

Acre

Elijah kills the prophets of Baal

The River Kishon which flows through the Valley of Jezreel near the banks of which Elijah met the priests, of Baal. Mount Carmel, where Elijah performed his miracle, in the background.

"And Elijah said unto them, take the prophets of Baal; let not one of them escape. And they took them: and Elijah brought them down to the brook Kishon, and slew them there." (1 Kings 18:40.)

The walls at Acre, looking through to the Mediterranean.

ALTHOUGH mentioned only casually in the Old and New Testaments, the ancient city of Acre has played an important role in the history of Palestine. No records remain to indicate when this old fortress city was established, yet, it is entirely probable that it was in existence when Abraham first traveled the length of the Promised Land from Haran to Beersheba.

In any event, by the time Joshua was engaged in his conquest of Palestine, Acre was an impregnable fortress which he could not subdue. When the land was divided among the tribes of Israel, Acre was in the area allotted to Asher, but he also failed to drive out the inhabitants of Accho (Acre) and "the Asherites dwelt among the Canaanites, inhabitants of the land." (Judges 1:31-32.)

Acre is located on the Mediterranean coast near the northern end of what is now Israel and immediately adjacent to the thriving city of Haifa. The Acre port surrounds a natural cove in one of the few sheltered harbors on this part of the Mediterranean coast. Back of the city stretch the Plains of Acre which provide a natural access to the interior —to Galilee, to ancient Gilead, and to Damascus. Down through the ages, Acre was the chief port of entry for this rich country.

The River Kishon flows through the Acre plain and into the Mediterranean. Old Testament students will remember that it was on the River Kishon that the Prophetess Deborah defeated the Canaanites in one of the famous Old Testament battles. It was on the banks of this river, also, that the Prophet Elijah killed the priests of Baal after he had humiliated them on the top of Mount Carmel—a few miles to the south—when their false god had failed to produce a requested miracle.

As a fortified harbor leading to such an important area, Acre has been a frequent target for would-be conquerors. Among those who sieged or who conquered the city were the Egyptians, Thutmose III, Seti I, and Rameses II. During the Assyrian Conquest, Acre felt the sword of Sennacherib, Esarhaddon, and Ashurbanipal. When the Greeks occupied Palestine, Alexander the Great conquered Acre and, later, the Greeks changed its name to Ptolemais, probably in honor of Ptolemy II—Philadelphus, king of Egypt, who ruled Palestine and fortified Akko (Acre), in 61 B.C.

During the life and times of Jesus, the Romans ruled and occupied this area, and it was at Acre that Herod the Great entertained Julius Caesar for whom he had named three Palestinian cities, Caesarea, Tiberias, and Sebaste. The only mention of Acre in the New Testament, however, is an account connected with Paul's travels in which he narrates "we came to Ptolemais, and saluted the brethren, and abode with them one day." (Acts 21:7.)

After the Christian era, Acre became an important port and fortress for the crusaders, the Moslems, the Turks and, finally, was reduced virtually to rubble when Napoleon invaded Palestine and attempted to conquer the fort. However, during this attack, the Turks solicited the help of the British and, backed by part of the British fleet, defeated Napoleon and forced him to leave Palestine.

By the time of World War I, Acre had decayed into virtual unimportance, and Haifa, the neighboring city, became administrative headquarters for the district under British rule.

Today, Acre, located adjacent to beautiful Haifa, has perhaps reached another turning point in its eventful history. Sharing in the growth and prosperity of its neighboring city, Acre also provides excellent tourist attractions. Its ancient walls and crusader ruins present a dramatic and romantic insight into the city's historic past. Moreover, recently the area was selected as the site for the filming of *Exodus*, which told the dramatic story of the birth of the sovereign state of Israel.

If Acre returns to a position of importance, it will not be in its old role as a Mediterranean fortress, but rather as an industrial and tourist center.

Ashkelon

ancient Philistine stronghold

Some of the ruins of ancient Ashkelon.

"How can it (the sword) be quiet, seeing the Lord hath given it a charge against Ashkelon, and against the sea shore? there hath he appointed it."
(Jeremiah 47: 7.)

Excavated pillars from an ancient Ashkelon building.

WHEN the Patriarch Abraham led his small group down from Haran into and through Canaan, undoubtedly he took great pains to skirt and keep his party at a safe distance from Ashkelon. Even in those ancient days, Ashkelon already had a reputation as a formidable city. As one of the five leading cities of the Philistines, Ashkelon, the main harbor city, was the Philistines' chief cultural center. Its leaders and people were fierce warriors and exceptionally hostile to strangers.

Even after Joshua's conquest of Canaan, the Philistines, centered at Ashkelon, still remained fiercely anti-Israel. It was primarily against these peoples that King Saul aimed his campaigns; and when Saul was killed, David his successor, warned: "... publish it not in the streets of Ashkelon; lest the daughters of the Philistines rejoice, lest the daughters of the uncircumcised triumph." (II Samuel 1:20.) David, undoubtedly, was well aware of the power still held by the Philistines and, at Saul's death, did not want to give his enemies any encouragement.

Some 600 years later, Ashkelon was still a serious threat to Israeli control. The Prophet Jeremiah, pleading with his people to cease conquests by the sword, said: "O thou sword of the Lord, how long will it be ere thou be quiet? put up thyself into thy scabbard, rest, and be still." Then, in answer to his own appeal, the prophet continued, "How can it be quiet, seeing the Lord hath given it a charge against Ashkelon, and against the sea shore? there hath he appointed it." (Jeremiah 47:6, 7.) Shortly before Jeremiah's appeal, the Prophet Amos had cursed the city of Ashkelon, saying, "Thus sayeth the Lord God, I will cut off the inhabitant from Ashdod and him that holdeth the sceptre from Ashkelon." The Prophet Zephaniah also had predicted the destruction of the city, saying, "For Gaza shall be forsaken, and Ashkelon a desolation. . . ." (Zephaniah 2:4.)

According to Josephus, in his *Antiquities of the Jews,* when King David, during his conquest of the whole Philistine area, conquered the coastal cities, including Ashkelon, this important city served for a season as the repository of the Ark of the Covenant. Thus it became a substantial Israeli city.

During the Roman occupation, the city was restored and rebuilt with splendid edifices. It is also believed that Herod the Great was born at Ashkelon, for he took a special, personal interest in rebuilding the city and making sure that it was magnificent.

During the Moslem domination, Ashkelon was the center of an area of great importance and one which resisted violently the invasion of the Crusaders. Many important crusader battles were fought in and around the city. After its conquest, Richard the Lion Hearted built a wall around Ashkelon, the foundations of which have been excavated and are still visible.

In the year A.D. 570, Antonius Martyr visited the city and spoke of certain Egyptians who had been killed there. A church had been erected in their memory, indicating that at one time Egypt controlled Ashkelon.

Archaeological explorations of the area began soon after the turn of the century. Yet, much still is to be discovered in this ancient city with such a troubled and heroic past.

During recent years, a special type of onion, named in Latin, *ascalonia*, was grown and developed in Ashkelon. This is the original specie of our onions now known as escallions.

Avdat

resting place for
Moses and the Children of Israel

A part of the court and ruins of Avdat, an ancient Nabatean community on the borders of the Valley of Zin.

"Then came the children of Israel, . . . into the desert of Zin in the first month: and the people abode in Kadesh; and Miriam died there, and was buried there." (Num. 20:1.)

Eyn Avdat—a spring of fresh water near the border of the Valley of Zin where the Children of Israel may have camped.

WHEN Moses led the Children of Israel from Sinai back toward the Promised Land, according to the Old Testament the pilgrimage traveled through the Valley of Zin. This great wilderness, or desert, lies south and east of the south end of the Dead Sea. It is a rugged, forbidding, and desolate area with no water except in a few isolated spots.

In all probability, when the Children of Israel traveled north through this wilderness, they must have turned east through the Valley of Zin and traveled up the east side of the Dead Sea to the area of Mount Nebo, near the north end of the sea, from which Moses could see the Land of Canaan. It will be recalled that Moses could look into the Promised Land from Mount Nebo, but he was forbidden by the Lord to enter it.

On the borders of the Wilderness of Zin, in the heart of Israel's Negev Desert, in a deep crevasse, is a well of cool, fresh water now known as Eyn Avdat. This is the only natural well in a wide expanse of desert and if this water were here at the time of Moses' journey, it could explain why the Children of Israel sojourned here and used this area as a camp site from which to explore the northern region to the border of the Promised Land.

The Old Testament account tells us that the Lord spoke to Moses here and instructed him to send a party of men (spies) to go north and search out the land of Canaan, "which I give unto the children of Israel." (Num. 13:2.)

Moses selected his men carefully and sent them into the country to learn about the people who dwelled there, whether they were strong or weak, few or many. He also wanted to learn what the land was like, whether it was good or bad, and where the strongholds of the people were located.

Only a short distance from the fresh water well, Eyn Avdat, on the top of a nearby hill, are the ruins of an ancient city. These ruins are now known as Avdat and give evidence of a flourishing community once occupied by an industrious people who had worked out an ingenious system of irrigation and water canals which served the city and also provided water for an extensive agricultural development.

The ruins of this city can be traced back to the Nabateans who are known to have lived in this area as early as the second century before Christ. Without doubt, life in this community was supported by water from the nearby well and also from rainfall which was carefully and ingeniously run through canals and into cisterns during the short periods of precipitation. This water was conserved for use during the long dry season. The Nabateans were a tribal people who had probably emigrated from Arabia and who, before the time of the Romans, had established a significant kingdom which extended over a wide area on the Sinai peninsula. Their capital was at Petra, which today is one of the most fantastic of the world's ancient ruins.

70 The ruins at Avdat, on which both the Romans

and the Byzantines had built cities, indicate that the community consisted of a fortress, monastery, baptistry, three churches, a wine press, a Roman military quarter, a commercial center and other community facilities. At one time Avdat could have supported several thousand people.

We do not know, of course, whether or not any community existed in this area at the time of the sojourn of Moses and the Children of Israel. Moreover, we are not sure whether the existence of the pool of fresh water can be traced back as far as this period. Nevertheless, the fact that this is the only available water in this wide area, plus the biblical record that the Children of Israel passed through this area and resided for a period here, provide credence to the possibility that this could have been the place where Moses and the Children of Israel rested.

If the Avdat area was a resting place for the pilgrimage of the Children of Israel, this was where Miriam, Moses' older sister, died and was buried. It will be remembered that it was Miriam who watched over the baby Moses when he was hidden in the bulrushes on the River Nile. She, also, became a prophetess among the Children of Israel and led the congregational singing of hallelujahs when Moses and the Children of Israel had successfully crossed the Red Sea and evaded the pursuing Egyptians.

The ruins of Avdat are located approximately

35 miles south of Beersheba on the new paved road which now runs from central Israel, through Beersheba and on to Elath, on the Gulf of Aqaba on the Red Sea. Avdat is one of the most completely excavated and one of the most interesting ruins in Israel. It was first discovered in 1871 by a British traveler who came upon it by chance. In 1935 a small-scale archaeological excavation was undertaken, but the complete ruins were not excavated until during the past few years. The community takes its name from Obodas (Avdat) the II, king of the Nabateans, who lived contemporarily with King Herod and was buried here.

The community was probably near its peak of activity and importance during the lifetime and ministry of Jesus of Nazareth. Of course, there is no evidence and it is not likely that Jesus ever visited the community. His influence, however, later permeated Avdat as indicated by the number of Christian relics, inscriptions and other religious artifacts that have been found here.

Remains of an old Roman fort near the Valley of Zin. Avdat's unique agricultural system in the background.

Beersheba

home of Abraham, Isaac, and Jacob

Bedouin tent in Israel similar to those in which the patriarchs lived.

"So Abraham returned unto his
young men and they rose up and
went together to Beersheba; and
Abraham dwelt at Beersheba."
(Gen. 22:19.)

The camel market in Beersheba, probably the only one of its kind in the world.

BEFORE the great patriarch Abraham died and was buried in Machpelah, he moved his flocks and possessions south from Hebron to Beersheba, the land bordering the desert where he dug a well and planted a grove. In all probability, he was already acquainted with this country, having traveled through it on his way to and from Egypt, during the period of the famine in Canaan.

After Abraham's death, his son Isaac resettled Beersheba, reopened his father's wells, and prospered here. In fact, so great was his prosperity as a farmer and herdsman, that the Philistines who possessed the land were extremely jealous of him. Their envy was so intense that Isaac was forced to take his family and possessions and move further south to Gerar, near Gaza, for a brief sojourn.

Returning to Beersheba after the Philistines' envy had subsided, Isaac and his servants dug another well and made a friendly covenant with Abimelech, king of the Philistines. This agreement permitted the patriarch to remain in his father's country. The well Isaac dug was called Shebah, meaning "an oath." The name of the town which grew up around this well was Beersheba, meaning "the well of the oath."

Isaac grew old, and his eyes grew dim while he resided at Beersheba. It was under these circumstances that he was led to give his patriarchal blessing to his son Jacob rather than to Esau, his firstborn.

It will be remembered that the two boys were

twins but Easu was the firstborn. Rebekah, their mother, loved Jacob more than Esau and was determined that he should receive his father's inheritance. She arranged the deception which brought Isaac's choice blessings to Jacob after Esau had sold his birthright to his brother.

Isaac's family grew up in and around Beersheba but when the sons were old enough to marry, Esau took a Philistine woman for a wife. Isaac and Rebekah then insisted that Jacob leave this country and return to the land of their family, Haran, there to find his wife.

On his trip from Beersheba to Haran, Jacob stopped overnight at Bethel. There he had the wonderful vision of a ladder which extended into heaven on which he saw angels and the Lord ascending and descending. There, also, Jacob received the blessings promised to his fathers that "through him all the nations of the world would be blessed."

After this blessing, Jacob covenanted with the Lord to return to him one tenth of all the Lord would give him. Jacob consecrated the place with an altar as had his grandfather, Abraham, before him.

At Haran, Jacob met his mother's brother Laban and, after working for him for many years, was given Laban's daughters Leah and Rachel in marriage. From these two great women and from their two maid servants came the twelve sons who became the patriarchs of the House of Israel.

On his return south to his father's homeland in

Hebron, Jacob crossed the brook Jabbok and there wrestled all night with an angel. In the morning, the angel blessed him and changed his name to Israel, saying, "Thy name shall be called no more Jacob, but Israel: for as a prince hast thou power with God and with men, and hast prevailed." (Gen. 32:28.)

The river Jabbok is in the general vicinity of Shechem and Dothan where Jacob's sons herded his flocks and where Joseph's brothers sold him to the owners of a caravan who took him to Egypt. According to the Old Testament story, Jacob had sent his son Joseph from the Valley of Hebron to check on his brothers at Shechem to see how they were getting along. Their jealousy and envy for the younger brother, whom Jacob so loved, prompted the brothers to plot to kill him. But when Reuben and Judah objected, they agreed to sell him into the Egyptian caravan.

Not only was Beersheba a home of the patriarchs, it was also visited by other Old Testament kings and prophets. During the period of his frequent flights from the anger of King Saul, David is believed to have spent some time in refuge at Beersheba.

The prophet Elijah also spent some time in hiding at Beersheba. After he had confounded the priests of Baal on Mount Carmel, and had them killed, Elijah fled to Beersheba and sought refuge there.

Beersheba (Beer-Shev'a in Hebrew) presently

is the capital of the Negev and the gateway to the great desert. The town's population is entirely Jewish, most of whom are immigrants who have recently come to Israel from many parts of the world.

During the 1948 Palestinian War, decisive battles were fought at Beersheba. Also, during World War I, under the leadership of General Allenby, Beersheba was the first city in Palestine captured from the Turks by the British.

As a gateway to the desert, Beersheba is an assembly place for the thousands of Bedouins who reside in and roam over the desert. The Negev Desert sustains approximately 13,000 Bedouins whose chief means of livelihood comes from the breeding of cattle and camels. Beersheba has become a central market place for these Bedouins who converge on the city for a weekly market which opens at dawn every Thursday morning. Here these Bedouins buy, sell, and exchange camels, sheep, goats, poultry, farm produce, and an interesting variety of homemade products, including sweets, bakery items, hand-hammered metals, and hand-woven fabrics. The Beersheba market is probably the only one of its kind in the world.

Beersheba is one of modern Israel's most interesting and historic places. As modern irrigation gradually pushes the desert back, Beersheba is destined to play an important part in the rebirth and redevelopment of Israel's part of the Holy Land.

A Bedouin couple leading their camel away from the market at Beersheba.

Bethlehem

most blessed among cities

Part of the Church of the Nativity believed to have been built over the stable where Jesus was born.

"And Joseph also went up from Galilee, out of the city of Nazareth, into Judea, unto the city of David, which is called Bethlehem; . . . To be taxed with Mary his espoused wife, being great with child." (Luke 2:4-5.)

The courtyard of the Church of the Nativity. The elderly priest is a caretaker.

AND IT CAME to pass in those days, that there went out a decree from Caesar Augustus, that all the world should be taxed. . . .

"And all went to be taxed, every one into his own city.

"And Joseph also went up from Galilee out of the city of Nazareth, into Judaea, unto the city of David, which is called Bethlehem . . . To be taxed with Mary his espoused wife, being great with child.

"And so it was, that while they were there, the days were accomplished that she should be delivered.

"And she brought forth her firstborn son, and wrapped him in swaddling clothes, and laid him in a manger; because there was no room for them in the inn." (Luke 2:1-7.)

Hundreds of years before this glorious event, the prophet Micah foresaw that this little city had been chosen as a place for the Savior's birth. "But thou, Bethlehem . . . though thou be little among the thousands of Judah, yet out of thee shall he come forth unto me that is to be ruler in Israel; whose goings forth have been from of old, from everlasting." (Micah 5:2.)

This prediction, too, became the source of Herod's information when he sent the wise men to Bethlehem to inquire about Jesus' birth and to bring news about him.

According to the Jewish historian, Flavius Josephus, shortly before the time of Jesus' birth, a rumor had spread throughout the area that the Lord had decided to bring the Roman rule to an end and a new king would be born who would rule Judaea. This news greatly disturbed the aging and jealous Herod. He gathered the chief priests and scribes together and asked them where Christ would be born. It was then that they quoted to him Micah's prophecy. Secretly, he sent the wise men to Bethlehem and said, "Go and search diligently for the young child; And when ye have found him, bring me word again, that I may come and worship him also." (Matt. 2:8.)

The story is well known how the wise men found the Christ Child and, after worshiping him and giving him gifts, an angel appeared to them in a dream and warned them not to go back and report to Herod. Herod, in his wrath, then ordered that all children in Bethlehem, two years old and under, should be slain. Thus, he fulfilled also another prophecy made hundreds of years earlier by Jeremiah, the prophet, when he said, "Thus saith the Lord; A voice was heard in Ramah, lamentation, and bitter weeping; Rachel weeping for her children refused to be comforted for her children, because they were not." (Jeremiah 31:15.)

Bethlehem has been a chosen city from patriarchal days. It was near the present town, on the road from Jerusalem to Hebron, that Jacob's beloved Rachel was buried. It will be recalled that

A portion of the field where shepherds were abiding with their flocks.

she died while giving birth to her second son, Benjamin, and the saddened Jacob took her body to these pleasant hills for burial. Her tomb can still be visited on the outskirts of the little town of Bethlehem.

As early as the time of the Judges, Bethlehem was a specially honored place. At this time, a good man named Elimelech of the Tribe of Judah lived at Bethlehem. He and his wife, Naomi, had two sons. Because food was scarce in Judaea, he took his family and moved to the east of the Dead Sea into the land of Moab. There, his two sons married Moabite women; one was Ruth. Soon thereafter, Elimelech and his two sons died, and the bereaved Naomi decided she should return to the land of her fathers. It was under these circumstances that the beautiful story of Ruth's great love and devotion unfolded. Her mother-in-law had suggested that she and her sister-in-law remain in the land of her people, the Moabites. So deep, however, was Ruth's love for her mother-in-law that she insisted on returning to Judaea, saying, "Intreat me not to leave thee, or to return from following after thee: for whither thou goest, I will go; and where thou lodgest I will lodge: thy people shall be my people, and thy God my God." (Ruth 1:16.)

All Bible students know the sequel to this beautiful story. Naomi and Ruth returned to Bethlehem, and there Ruth met and married the rich Boaz. They had a son named Obed and he, in turn, was the father of Jesse, who was the father of David, who became king of all Israel.

It was at Bethlehem that Samuel the Prophet came on direct instructions of the Lord to seek out the young boy, David, and anoint him to become king of Israel. David and his brothers lived and grew up in Bethlehem. He was here with his father when he was sent with food and gifts to his older brothers, who were at the battlefield fighting the Philistines. While at the front, David learned of the giant Goliath, who was challenging and threatening the Israelites. He persuaded King Saul to permit him to go out and accept the giant's challenge. Then followed the historic fight between David and Goliath which changed the whole trend of the war and established David as the man destined to take the reins of leadership from Saul's faltering hands.

David spent a considerable amount of time in Bethlehem and had many experiences there. After Saul's death and after he became king, Bethlehem became known as the City of David. It became a holy city of sanctity and at one time housed the Ark of the Covenant. David wrote one of his psalms about it and described it as "a place for the Lord, an habitation for the mighty God of Jacob." (Psalm 132.)

It was because Joseph and Mary were both descendants of the House of David that they followed Herod's instructions and came up from their

89

home town of Nazareth to Bethlehem there to be enrolled on Herod's tax lists.

Because of the great events that transpired there, Bethlehem still retains its atmosphere of holiness. It is now a quaint, relatively small town—predominantly Christian—about six miles in direct distance from Jerusalem.

Adjacent to the city are the fields where, on that night, there were "shepherds abiding in the field, keeping watch over their flock by night.

"And, lo, the angel of the Lord came upon them, and the glory of the Lord shown round about them: and they were sore afraid.

"And the angel said unto them, Fear not: for behold, I bring you good tidings of great joy, which shall be to all people.

"For unto you is born this day, in the city of David, a Saviour, which is Christ the Lord." (Luke 2:8-11.)

Bethlehem is truly a blessed place. Worldwide Christians believe that the greatest event in the history of the world transpired in this humble little town.

Rachel's tomb on the road to Hebron near Bethlehem.

Bethany

Lazarus was raised from the dead

Bethany, a place Jesus loved to visit

"And he led them out as far as
to Bethany, and he lifted up his
hands, and blessed them."
(Luke 24:50.)

*The street in Bethany where Lazarus and his sisters
may have lived.*

BETHANY, situated about two miles from Jerusalem near the brow of the Mount of Olives, was a place where Jesus loved to visit. In the town lived three of Jesus' most beloved followers. Lazarus and his two sisters, Mary and Martha, were choice friends of Jesus and during his visits to Judea, their home was always open to him.

As recorded in the New Testament Gospels, Jesus performed many miracles throughout the land. Without doubt, however, his greatest miracle was performed at Bethany. This remarkable story is well known to all students of the New Testament. During the last year of his ministry, Jesus had visited Jerusalem many times. Shortly before the miracle at Bethany was performed, Jesus had been at Jerusalem during the period from the Feast of the Tabernacles in October to that of the dedication in December. He had, however, been driven out of the city and a crowd had followed him into the area of the Jordan. Here he was teaching and performing his many acts of mercy when he received word that his friend, Lazarus, was sick. Instead of returning immediately to Bethany, however, he remained among his followers for two days before beginning the journey back.

In the meantime, Lazarus had died from his sickness, and when Jesus arrived at Bethany, Lazarus' body had been laying in the tomb for some four days.

When Jesus met the sisters, both of them de-

clared unto him their sorrow and said that if he had
been there, their brother would not have died. It
was under these circumstances that Jesus made his
remarkable statement which has been such a source
of comfort to all who have lost loved ones. As recorded in the 11th chapter of the Gospel of John,
Jesus said, "I am the resurrection, and the life: he
that believeth in me, though he were dead, yet shall
he live:

"And whosoever liveth and believeth in me
shall never die." (John 11:25-26.)

Martha responded that she knew that her brother would rise in the resurrection, but Jesus assured
her that if she would only believe, her brother could
be raised from the dead.

Then occurred the remarkable miracle when
Jesus had the tomb opened and he called out to
Lazarus, in a loud voice, "Lazarus, come forth."
Then Lazarus, bound head, foot, and hand with
grave clothes, walked out of the tomb to the great
astonishment of a large group of mourners and
friends from Bethany and from Jerusalem who had
been at the home of Mary and Martha to comfort
them. According to John's account, it was this great
miracle, which had such profound effect upon the
people who witnessed it, that motivated the deter-
mination on the part of the authorities to set the
events in motion which culminated in Jesus' trial
and crucifixion.

Although the town of Bethany undoubtedly was

founded long before the time of Jesus, there is no mention of it in the Old Testament. A tradition exists, however, that Bethany earlier was the village of el-Azariyeh. The topography of the area strongly indicates that this is a real possibility.

The small town is known, however, primarily for the experiences as described above and as a preferred resting place for Jesus and some of his disciples. It was from here that the procession originated when Jesus and his disciples marched triumphantly into Jerusalem just before the Last Supper, the betrayal, and the crucifixion. Bethany, or very near here, is also believed to be the place, according to Luke, chapter 24, where Jesus' ascension took place. Although exact location cannot be certain, the house where Lazarus, Mary, and Martha lived is pointed out to visitors. The tomb where Lazarus was laid is also identified. However, it is highly doubtful that these are the exact places.

Bethel

sacred place of sacrifice

A ruin at Bethel near where Abraham built an altar.

"And Jacob rose up early in the
morning, and took the stone that
he had put for his pillows, and
set it up for a pillar, and poured
oil upon the top of it. And he
called the name of that place
Bethel." (Gen. 28:18-19.)

The hills near Bethel where Jacob wrestled with the angels.

WHEN Abraham, obeying the instructions of the Lord, left Haran and took his small group into Canaan, he made camp on a high, rocky hill and there built an altar and offered a sacrifice to his God. This account, recorded in the 12th chapter of Genesis, is the first mention of Bethel, this interesting place destined to become a sacred site for the Israelites and mentioned more often in the Bible than any other city except Jerusalem.

When Isaac's servants journeyed from Beersheba back through Canaan to Haran to find a wife for their master, Isaac, they, too, undoubtedly camped overnight at this site. One of the more renowned incidents that occurred here, however, involved Jacob. He, too, was instructed to travel back to Haran, the original home of the family, there to find a wife for himself. As he and his entourage journeyed north through the Canaanite country, he camped on the mountain at Bethel. It was here that he had his remarkable dream in which he saw a ladder stretching down from the sky on which angels were traveling back and forth from the earth into heaven. At the top of the ladder, Jacob dreamed that he saw the Lord himself, who reiterated to him the blessings given to his father, Isaac, and to his grandfather, Abraham, that this land would be his and his family's and that he would be blessed on his journey.

As recorded in Genesis, chapter 28, Jacob made a pillow out of smooth stones on which he laid his head when he received his memorable vision. Here, he made a vow with the Lord that if the Lord would protect him as he had promised, he would keep the Lord's commandments and would return to him a tenth (tithe) of all of the material things with which he was blessed. Apparently, during the years since Abraham's visit, the Canaanites had given the place the new name of Luz. Jacob renamed the place Bethel, which, in Hebrew, means House of the Lord, or God's House.

Bethel is located some 12 miles north of Jerusalem near the town now called Beitin. The village obtains its water, as anciently, from four springs which nourish the area. Many important biblical events occurred in this area. After Solomon's death when the kingdom was divided between Jeroboam and Rehoboam into the two warring factions of Judah and Israel, Jeroboam, king of Israel, built a temple here to rival the one that had been built in Jerusalem. The area then became a great sanctuary for the northern kingdom.

The prophetess Deborah had her home here somewhere between Bethel and Ramah. (Judges 4:5.) The prophet Samuel also sat as judge here and visited the area once every year. Perhaps in an effort to combat the growing influence of the calf-worshipping pagans who gained a foothold in Bethel, a school of the prophets was established here and the prophets Amos and Hosea visited the city and spent a considerable amount of time in the city. In fact, one of Amos' great sermons was delivered here. In this sermon, the Prophet testified:

"Surely the Lord God will do nothing, but he revealeth his secret unto his servants the prophets." (Amos 3:7.)

He also predicted:

"Behold, the days come, saith the Lord God, that I will send a famine in the land, not a famine of bread, nor of thirst for water, but of hearing the words of the Lord:

"And they shall wander from sea to sea, and from the north even to the east they shall run to and fro to seek the word of the Lord, and shall not find it." (Amos 8:11-12.)

As was so characteristic of many of these ancient biblical cities, Bethel changed hands many times. Although the Arc of the Covenant was brought here by the Israelites, the city at one time had been a royal Canaanite community. Its earliest recorded settled occupation was around 2000 B.C. At one time it was conquered by the Egyptians and in the fourth century B.C. by the Greeks. The Roman Vaspasian conquered it on his march to Jerusalem.

Extensive archaeological excavations at the site were begun in 1934 by a group under the direction of Dr. Albright. This dig uncovered the foundations of a high-quality city which gave evidence of great architectural skill. This was later covered by a much coarser type of construction, indicating not only a less highly developed civilization but also the procedure, so pronounced throughout these Bible lands, of an original city being destroyed and another being built over its foundations.

Caesarea

city of ancient magnificence

...cavated courtyard at Caesarea where Paul may have been brought before Agrippa.

*"Then Agrippa said unto Paul,
Almost thou persuadest me to be
a Christian. And Paul said, I
would to God that not only thou,
but all that hear me this day,
were both almost, and altogether
such as I am . . ."* (Acts 26:28-
29.)

Ruins of the huge mole which protected the large Caesarea harbor.

THE infamous House of Herod, which ruled Palestine so long and during such a critical period, did many things to make secure its place in history. Along with the intrigue and cruelty, so much a part of this family's reign, it is an interesting fact that both Herod the Great and his son, Herod Antipas, were builders of magnificent cities and recreation areas. The ruins of their genius for construction stretch from Jerusalem to Tiberias on the Sea of Galilee through the now old excavated town of Sebastia and on down the Israel coast to Caesarea.

Caesarea was one of the most beautiful cities and was at the peak of its glory during the lifetime of Jesus. Caesarea was rebuilt by Herod the Great on an ancient Canaanite site on the Mediterranean coast between Joppa and Dora—now approximately 25 miles north of Tel Aviv. Herod took twelve years to build the city and celebrated its completion (B.C. 10-9) with spectacular games and riotous entertainment which at that time cost the equivalent of $300,000.

The city consisted of a large harbor protected by a huge mole and surrounded with a high wall topped with ten lofty towers.

In the city was an elaborately ornate temple to Augustus Caesar—for whom the city was named. Also included was a huge hippodrome and an outside amphitheater capable of seating 20,000 people.

Water was brought into the city through an intricate and extremely clever engineering system of aqueducts—one of which was eight miles long and stretched back to a spring in the hills of Palestine. The city was laid out and the drainage so planned as to allow the tides to roll in and flush out the streets which lay immediately adjacent to the coast.

Caesarea was the official residence of the Roman procurators, including Pontius Pilate. It was from here that Pilate went when he took up temporary residence in Jerusalem at the time of the trial which led to the crucifixion of Jesus. It was here also that Pilate ordered the massacre of the Jews who had come down from Jerusalem to protest the presence of profane eagle standards and the images of the Emperor which had been placed in and around the temple in Jerusalem. When these emissaries proved that they were willing to sacrifice their lives in an effort to accomplish their mission, Pilate revoked the order and removed the images.

It is believed that Philip was the first to preach Christianity at Caesarea, and it was here that Paul was brought before Agrippa and that, as a result of his masterful and stirring testimony, Agrippa remarked, "Almost thou persuadest me to be a Christian." It was also at Caesarea, under Felix, that Paul was imprisoned for two years.

Cornelius was a centurion at Caesarea. He was a God-fearing, devout man who prayed constantly for guidance. In answer to his prayers, Cornelius had a vision in which he was told to summon Peter, who was then at Joppa at the home of Simon the tanner.

Up to this time, the gospel had been preached only to the Jews. However, prior to meeting with Cornelius' messengers, Peter, too, had a vision in which he saw a great sheet descending from heaven on which were all manner of four-footed beasts of the earth and other creeping things which Peter believed were not fit to eat. Yet, he was commanded to kill and eat.

From this manifestation, Peter learned that the gospel was for everyone and not only for the Jews. Consequently, he accompanied the messengers back to Caesarea where he baptized Cornelius and those of his household and friends who had assembled themselves together. Following this baptism, the Holy Ghost fell upon the whole body of the Gentiles assembled with Cornelius, thus inaugurating the gentile Pentecost.

After almost a decade of sumptuous glory, Caesarea began its rapid decline under the wickedness of the last procurator, Florus. His cruel policies drove the Jews into revolt, and a riot in Caesarea brought about the massacre of 20,000 Jews there and led to the uprising in Jerusalem which initiated its destruction—69 A.D. Even in this final tragic drama, however, Caesarea played its important part. The city was used as the base of operations from which Jerusalem was destroyed.

Under the present program of archaeological excavations sponsored by the Israel government, the

Hebrew University, and with the assistance of funds from universities and foundations all over the world, the ruins of Caesarea and other important biblical sites have been excavated or are currently in the process of excavation. During the past few years, the Caesarea area has been a beehive of activity with crews of workers operating modern equipment under the supervision of careful archaeologists. In one section of the ruins, a huge steam shovel has been at work piling up large mounds of debris from which all kinds of fantastic artifacts are recovered. In other areas, archaeologists with hand tools and soft brushes have carefully removed the soil and the dust from precious statues, bas-reliefs, and huge foundation stones on which clear, decipherable inscriptions can be read.

From the pottery, the coins, the marble statues and columns and from the inscriptions, scholars of ancient Hebrew can read again, with remarkable accuracy, the wonderful and tragic history of this once magnificent city.

As the ruins are brought to light and as the foundations of the various buildings take shape, this spectacular shrine is rapidly becoming one of the wonders of the archaeological world. Many thousands of visitors have already walked through this ancient city. In the future, countless thousands more will come with their thoughts and imaginations running back through the ages to both the glory and shame which once were so much a part of Caesarea.

Excavated ruins of huge outside amphitheater at the site of ancient Caesarea.

Caesarea Philippi

"whom do men say that I am?"

The Jordan River near its source at Caesarea-Philippi.

And Jesus went out, and his disciples, unto the towns of Caesarea-Philippi.

Crusader Ruins at Caesarea-Philippi.

THE history of the country adjacent to Caesarea Philippi reaches far back into antiquity. To the Christians, however, this northern-most section of Israel has a special significance.

The three synoptic gospels, Matthew, Mark, and Luke, all record the occasion when Jesus and his disciples visited the coasts of Caesarea Philippi and Jesus asked his disciples, "Whom do men say that I the Son of man am?" The Gospels record their answer: "Some say that thou art John the Baptist: some, Elias; and others, Jeremias, or one of the prophets."

Jesus then asked, "But whom say ye that I am? And Simon Peter answered and said, Thou art the Christ, the Son of the living God." (Matthew 16:13-16, Mark 8:27, Luke 9:18-20.)

It is recorded that Jesus' response to Peter was that flesh and blood had not revealed this to him but that this information had come by revelation from his Father in heaven. Jesus further told his disciples that his Church would be built upon this rock of revelation. (Matthew 16:13-19.) This is one of the important recorded statements in the scriptures where Jesus affirmed his knowledge that he was the long-expected Messiah about whom the prophets had testified. Furthermore, this is a specific record of the acceptance by his disciples that Jesus was the long awaited Savior and Christ. Consequently, this area is a particularly hallowed one for the Christians.

Shortly before the time of Jesus, Herod the Great received the territory from Augustus. This was in approximately 20 B.C. and Herod erected a temple at the present site of Caesarea Philippi. The name of this area at that time was Paneas, and it was a sanctuary of the god of Greek mythology, Pan. Students of Greek mythology will remember that Pan was the god of fields, forests, wild animals, flocks, and shepherds and was represented with the legs, horns, and ears of a goat on a stylized body of a man.

Herod's son, Philip, rebuilt the city and changed its name from Paneas to Caesarea in honor of Augustus Caesar, but he added his own name to distinguish the town from the city his father, Herod, had established on the Mediterranean coast.

During the administration of Titus, he celebrated the capture of Jerusalem with gladiatorial shows in the arena at Caesarea Philippi. The city was later captured, in 1130, by the Crusaders and was finally lost by them to the Moslems in 1165. The region is relatively high, some 1,150 feet in altitude, and has bounteous water. In fact, one of the tributaries to the Jordan flows out of the base of Mount Hermon into a gushing stream and then through a deep crevasse as one of the headwaters of the Jordan.

Anciently, the region surrounding Caesarea Philippi was the section of Palestine assigned to the Tribe of Dan. The region borders on the foothills of Mount Hermon where some believe Jesus experienced his transfiguration. It is the section from which the headwaters combine to form the Jordan River. Tradition preserves the legend that anciently there were three streams flowing in different directions. A dispute broke out among them as to which was the biggest and the most important, and the legend records that the Lord, himself, hearing their dispute, descended and instructed them to unite into one big river. The hill upon which the Lord is supposed to have stood is still known as the Hill of the Judge, and the legendary story has produced the symbol of *strength through unity* among the people of Israel.

The name Jordan is believed to have derived from two sources, Jor and Dan, which combine to make the name Jordan. The river flows through exceedingly deep gorges to form the small lake of Hula and then passes on into the larger lake now known as Galilee.

The country surrounding Caesarea Philippi is rugged and beautiful. Mount Hermon, with its snowcapped peaks, provides an impressive background for the area, and not too far to the west and south is the beautiful and mystical city of Tsefat.

Capernaum

where Jesus began his ministry

The Sea of Galilee looking through the portico of one of the religious edifices on the top of the Mount of Beatitudes.

"And seeing the multitudes, he went up into a mountain: and when he was set, his disciples came unto him: And he opened his mouth, and taught them . . ."
(Matt. 5:1-2.)

Intricate stone carvings believed to be of the Arc of the Covenant (arrow) found among Capernaum ruins.

THE sparkling Sea of Galilee and its beautiful surrounding country was a choice and preferred area for Jesus. Although he was reared at Nazareth, he preferred Capernaum and its attractive setting near a hill overlooking the blue waters of Galilee. It was here that he began his ministry and probably preached his first sermon. It was from this area that he selected his first disciples, for, as recorded, "Jesus, walking by the sea of Galilee, saw two brethren, Simon called Peter, and Andrew his brother, casting a net into the sea: for they were fishers.

"And he saith unto them, Follow me, and I will make you fishers of men."

Going on a little farther, Jesus met James and John, his brother, whom he also called. Without argument or question, these fishermen "straightway left their nets, and followed him.

"And Jesus went about all Galilee, teaching in their synagogues and peaching the gospel of the kingdom, and healing all manner of sickness and all manner of disease among the people." (Matt. 5:18-23.)

During the lifetime and ministry of Jesus of Nazareth, there were a number of beautiful and important cities located on the shores of Galilee. Among these were Tiberias and Magdala, where Jesus' faithful and devoted follower, Mary Magdalene, was born. Other cities on the lake were Bethsaida, Gergesa, and Hippos. Of all these, Jesus preferred Capernaum and made this city his head-quarters during his ministry.

It will be recalled from the scriptures that after preaching in and around Capernaum, Jesus returned to his home town of Nazareth and, on the Sabbath day, entered the synagogue. Following the custom, he stood up among his friends and relatives and read a scripture from Isaiah which he said was being fulfilled in him. This statement so enraged his Nazarene friends that they took him out to a cliff, not far from the city, and would have thrown him over it, but he escaped and returned to Capernaum. It was on this occasion that Jesus made the remark, "No prophet is accepted in his own country."

At the time of Jesus' ministry, Capernaum stood on the main highway which ran from the Mediter-ranean coast into northern Trans-Jordan and Syria. It was a city of importance and was provided with a customs house and a military guard.

Due to its strategic significance, Capernaum was probably a busy and a cosmopolitan place with its fair share of both the poor and the sick. It was to these that Jesus went—healing and comforting them. It was probably from Capernaum that Jesus walked to a nearby mount and there gave his wonderful sermon on the Beatitudes. In all likeli-hood, also, it was back to Capernaum, or to a nearby area that, after his resurrection, Jesus instructed his disciples to meet him in Galilee.

Despite all this, Capernaum did not remain a

A group of ancient grinding mills at the site of Capernaum.

blessed city. Even with its miracles and healings, and in the face of the Lord's intimate presence in the city, he predicted that, because of its wickedness, it would be destroyed. He upbraided the people of Capernaum, saying: "And thou, Capernaum, which art exalted unto heaven, shalt be brought down to hell: for if the mighty works, which have been done in thee, had been done in Sodom, it would have remained until this day. But I say unto you, That it shall be more tolerable for Sodom in the day of judgment, than for thee." (Matt. 11:23-24.)

Capernaum's history moves from humility to glory and then to shame and destruction. The name Capernaum is a Greek corruption of the Hebrew name "Kefar-Nahum" (Village of Nahum).

According to Jewish tradition, Capernaum was the home of the Prophet Nahum, whose burial took place here at approximately 700 B.C.

Capernaum apparently developed into an important city prior to the Christian era and was beautified during the Roman period. After Christ's time, however, as he predicted, it degenerated and was completely out of existence by the sixth century, our time, and its ruins became merely a mound of earth. The city was never rebuilt nor were its ruins used to construct another. The site was purchased in 1894 by the Franciscans, who cleared the ruins and partly restored the ancient synagogue.

Today, the ruins of Capernaum provide proof of what once was its glory. The remains of the beautiful synagogue, possibly constructed after the time of Jesus, give evidence both of wealth and artistic application of architectural skill.

Other ruins now visible on the site of Caper-

The ruins of the synagogue at Capernaum, probably built after the time of Christ.

naum show magnificent carvings and intricate designs which reveal extreme care and skill in the construction of the important buildings which once graced this beautiful site and city—a place where Jesus so loved to be. **125**

Gath

ancient home of Goliath

The Valley of Elah, looking down from where it is believed Israel's armies were arrayed when David fought Goliath.

"And there went out a champion out of the camp of the Philistines, named Goliath, of Gath, whose height was six cubits and a span." (1 Sam. 17:4.)

The Tell of Gath. A tell is an archaeological mound formed over the ages by new cities being built on the ruins of old ones. This tell is being excavated.

DURING the reign of David, Israel began to reach the heights of her power and glory. It was in the Valley of Elah, only a few miles from the city of Gath, that David met and slew Goliath and first demonstrated the power that was to lead Israel to her great successes.

Everyone acquainted with the Bible is familiar with the story of the famous battle between David and Goliath. Although the details of the conflict are well known, only a few Bible scholars, however, believe they know where this unique battle took place.

It was approximately in the year 1063 B.C. that an over-confident, haughty giant stepped out in front of the Philistine army and for 40 days taunted the armies of Israel, arrayed on the other side of the valley, to send forth a warrior to do battle against him. His challenge was that if he were overpowered by the Israelite warrior, then all of the Philistines would become servants to the Israelites. On the other hand, if he were victorious, the Israelites would become their slaves.

The giant who threw this challenge was Goliath from Gath. He was, in height, 6 cubits and a span (an estimated 9 feet six inches) with a fully armored proportionate physique.

Almost by chance, David was visiting the Israelite armies under command of King Saul. David had come to bring provisions to his three brothers, who were at the battlefield. When he heard Goliath's challenge, he offered to fight him. The story of what happened as a result of a well-placed sling shot is well known. What has not been known is where this important action in the history of Israel took place.

The city of Gath is mentioned many times in the Old Testament. It was one of the five (Pentapolis) Philistine cities—the others being Gaza, Ashkelon, Ashdod and Ekron. Gath is called the Royal Philistine City and, consequently, must have been the abode of the Philistine kings. It was certainly the home of one of these kings during the period when David was fleeing from the anger of Saul, for he and his men took refuge in the city and lived there under the protection of one of the Philistine kings for a period of 16 months.

In addition to having been the home of Goliath and one of the places of refuge for David, Gath was sufficiently important to have been one of the cities into which the Ark of the Covenant was brought. The city played an important role throughout the reigns of Saul, David and Solomon. Later, Rehoboam fortified it and, still later, Amos tells of some great calamity that befell it. (Amos 6:2.)

Where was this important Philistine city and what happened to it?

For more than 25 years, archaeologists in the Holy Land have sought the site of ancient Gath. An intensive search was conducted during 1958-59 by R. H. Mitchell and Dr. B. Mazar, who, from literary research and on-the-spot investigations, came to the conclusion that a mound known as Tel en-Najila is, without reasonable doubt, the site of this famous old city. On-the-spot excavations have uncovered an impressive fortress which dates from the eighth century B.C. together with many artifacts and ruins which had established the site as an important archaeological area.

Excavations in earnest were began late in 1962 and were conducted for a period of at least five years. During the first year, excavations of the old fortress were completed and then a trial trench was dug to discover the extent of the history of the site. Since that time exploration has continued with significant success.

Archaeological technique, once the exploratory trench has been completed and the detailed plans outlined, is that each year actual field excavations are conducted for approximately two and a half months. The remainder of the time is used to classify the findings, decipher the possible inscriptions, and publish, in progressive reports, the results. This is the technique that was followed at Gath.

The excavations at the Gath Tell are under the supervision of Negev Biblical Excavations, Inc. The project has been approved to receive grants from the United States State Department and by the State of Israel. Princeton Theological Seminary is associated with the educational aspects of the project.

131

Financial participation in biblical excavations in Israel is being encouraged on the part of educational institutions and governments outside of Israel through a plan of generous participation in the ownership of artifacts discovered. The chief reason why so many U. S. universities have assisted in these excavations is that through this plan they have been able to take many valuable artifacts back to their museums for study and exposition.

It will be extremely interesting to learn what yet might be discovered during the excavations at Gath. This is the first extensive exploration of a Philistinian site, and from it much has been and may still be learned about a period in biblical and Israel history which up to the present has remained comparatively obscure.

Excavations at the Tell of Gath with modern Gath in background.
(Photo Courtesy of Israel Government Tourist Office.)

Hazor

last obstacle to Joshua's conquest

Excavations at Hazor showing ancient walls. Snow covered Mount Hermon in the background.

"But as for the cities that stood still in their strength, Israel burned none of them, save Hazor only; that did Joshua burn."
(Joshua 11:13.)

Additional excavations at Hazor with unexcavated mound (tell) in background.

FTER Joshua's successful siege of Jericho and his capture of the great city of Ai, his fame as a warrior spread rapidly throughout all the land of Canaan. Some of the tribes that occupied the land, fearing the Israelites, made peace with Joshua. Others, however, combined their forces to resist his advance into their country. Among these were the kings of Jerusalem, Hebron, Jarmuth, Lachish, and Eglon. In fact, these kings conspired against Gibeon because this tribe had made peace with Joshua.

The people of Gibeon called for Joshua's help, and together they utterly defeated these other kings and took over all of the southern part of Canaan, except the heights of Jerusalem itself. It was during this great battle at Gibeon that Joshua commanded the sun and the moon to stand still, and they obeyed, giving him more time to complete his conquest.

Joshua's fame and the fear of him now spread throughout the entire land from Dan to the north to Beersheba to the south.

The leader of the tribes to the north was Jabin, king of Hazor. When Jabin learned of Joshua's conquests, he contacted all of the kings in the area and formed a great coalition army near the waters of Merom, the small lake later known as Hula, north of the Sea of Galilee. Joshua heard of the kings' encampment, and before they could become fully organized, marched his armies up the Jordan Valley and attacked and conquered them. After this great victory, virtually the whole of the land of Canaan —the land promised to Abraham, Isaac, and Jacob, and to Moses—lay at Joshua's feet. After these conquests had been consolidated, peace came to the land, and it was divided among the Twelve Tribes.

Hazor, before the time of Joshua, was probably one of the ancient Canaanite fortresses. Its name seems to derive from "Hatzer," meaning courtyard or enclosure, possibly for flocks and herds. The city apparently grew up around this enclosure and became a prominent one in Palestine's history.

After Joshua's conquest, in approximately 1450 B.C., the place became a part of the Land of Naphtali. Other references to Hazor in the Old Testament indicate that around the tenth century B.C., King Solomon made it one of his chariot towns. Part of the taxes Solomon imposed upon the Israelites were apparently used to build his establishment at Hazor. (1 Kings 9:15.)

The Old Testament also records that approximately in the year 732 B.C., Hazor fell into the hands of the conquering Assyrian king, Tiglath-Pileser. It was at the time of the great dispersion that this conqueror carried many of the Children of Israel into captivity. (2 Kings 15:29.)

There is no reference in the New Testament to Hazor. We can assume that during the time of the ministry of Jesus of Nazareth, the ruins of this old city and fort had long since been covered by the soil and vegetation of the ages and had become one of Palestine's mounds.

138   The present archaeological excavations of Hazor

(Hatsor) are located about seven miles north of Tsefat, adjacent to a paved highway that leads from the Sea of Galilee. The Tell of Hazor was first discovered in 1928 by a small expedition sent out by the University of Liverpool, England. In 1955, archaeological excavations were begun on the site by an expedition led by Yigael Yadin of the Hebrew University. The present mound, which overlooks the Sea of Galilee in the distance on the south and from which can be seen Mount Hermon to the north, consists of two distinct parts. The higher section was probably the fort. In it are excavations of walls, towers, and the remains of a fortified city. Here also is an old Canaanite altar, similar to the one at Megiddo.

Below the upper mound, or tell, are the remains of what once must have been the Hazor community, or lower city. In all likelihood, the inhabitants farmed the surrounding area and, when danger threatened, retired to within the walls of the fort on the upper mound for protection.

Hazor is one of Israel's ancient shrines. Many artifacts of great antiquity have been removed from the ruins. These old relics tell a story of the history of this ancient place which stretches back beyond Joshua's time to the inhabitants who may have been in the land when Abraham first entered it.

Hazor has played its important role in history, but it may be best remembered as the last major obstacle which Joshua was forced to overcome before the Israelites' conquest of the Promised Land.

Hebron

burial place of the patriarchs

The Mosque at Hebron built over the tomb of the patriarchs.

"And Jacob came unto Isaac his father unto Mamre, unto the city of Arbah, which is Hebron, where Abraham and Isaac sojourned." (Gen. 35:27.)

Road from Hebron to Beersheba that leads into Egypt.

APPROXIMATELY halfway between Jerusalem and Beersheba, on the old road that comes through Bethlehem and on into Egypt, is the picturesque, ancient city of Hebron. Over the centuries, this old town has played a significant role in many important events in religious history.

For hundreds of years Hebron was the home of the patriarchs. Abraham, Isaac, and Jacob and their wives drew water from Hebron's well, herded their flocks, tilled the soil and, eventually, were buried here. Joseph, who had been sold into Egypt, visited Hebron. David fled and sought refuge here and, later, marshalled and trained the forces at Hebron that he needed to capture Jerusalem.

In all probability, Joseph, Mary, and the Christ child, to escape the wrath of Herod, passed through and possibly stopped overnight in Hebron on their flight into Egypt. Surely, the old town has experienced its rich share of memorable historical events.

Close on to 4,000 years ago, Abram, on special instructions of the Lord, took his family and left his home in Ur of the Chaldees and traveled west toward a Promised Land. After a brief sojourn at Haran, believed to be near what is now the Syrian-Turkish border, Abram with his wife Sarai, his nephew Lot, and a number of converts he had made in Haran, traveled south into the land of the Canaanites.

Abram's first campsite was at Shechem where the

patriarch, true to his covenant to the Lord, built his altar. From there, the small party traveled farther south to Bethel, where another altar was constructed.

Owing to a famine in Canaan, Abram took his small party for a brief sojourn into Egypt to obtain food. Returning from Egypt, he came back to Bethel and then moved on south to the Plains of Mamre (Hebron) where he established a permanent residence.

In all probability, on his trip to and from Egypt, Abram and his party must have passed through the Plains of Mamre and decided, because of the availability of water there and the quality of the soil, that this would be a good place for a permanent residence.

After returning from Egypt and settling in Hebron, the two families separated, and Lot made his residence in Sodom, one of the cities of the valley of the Dead Sea. Soon thereafter, Sodom and the other plains cities were attacked by invading kings and Lot was taken prisoner. Abram immediately marshalled his small military force and overpowered these kings, restoring Lot's possessions to him and reestablishing him in the country.

As an indication of the remarkable character of this great patriarch, Abram refused to take any of the possessions of the vanquished kings as spoils of war; in fact, from the king of Sodom he would not take "a thread even to a shoe latchet." (Gen. 14:23.)

After returning from the battle of the kings of the plains, Abram, while residing at Hebron, met the great high priest Melchizedek, who brought him bread and wine and blessed him and to whom Abram paid tithes of all he had.

While residing at Hebron, Abram and Sarai were visited by angels who blessed them, changed their names to Abraham and Sarah, and promised them they would have a son and that their offspring would be as countless as the stars in the heavens.

On one occasion when Abraham was before his tent under the oak tree in Hebron, three men approached. Abraham, in his great hospitality, invited them to rest, wash their feet, and break bread with him. When they agreed, he prepared a feast for them.

Abraham then learned that they were sent from the Lord again to promise him that through him and his posterity all the nations of the world would be blessed. Also, these men said they had come to learn of the wickedness of Sodom and the cities of the Dead Sea plains and, if necessary, to destroy them.

Later, after Lot had been warned, and he and his immediate family had escaped from the city, Sodom and Gomorrah and two of the three other wicked cities in the valley of the Dead Sea were

145

destroyed. From his residence under the oak tree in Hebron, Abraham could see the smoke and the fire which had destroyed these wicked cities.

Abraham was living at Hebron when he was commanded by the Lord to take his son Isaac to a mountain known as Moriah, near Jerusalem, and there offer him in sacrifice. Obedient and faithful, Abraham followed explicitly the commandment of the Lord. Then unfolded one of the greatest stories of love, devotion and obedience recorded in the scriptures.

Abraham took his beloved son and would have offered him in sacrifice had not an angel interfered. Truly, Abraham "believed in the Lord, and [the Lord] counted it to him for righteousness." (Gen. 15:6.)

Abraham also was residing at Hebron when he sent his trusted servant back to Haran, where the family of his brother Nahor was still living, there to obtain a wife for Isaac. Bible students are acquainted with the beautiful story of how this servant met Rebekah, recognized her as the woman selected by the Lord to be Isaac's wife, and how she, with complete trust and faith, left her home and loved ones to go to a strange land, there to meet Isaac, to become the mother of Jacob and Esau, and the great, revered ancestor of the Children of Israel.

146   At Hebron, Abraham purchased from the sons

of Heth a field in which was located the cave of Machpelah. Here, he buried his beloved wife, Sarah, and consecrated this old cave as his private family burial place.

At the ripe old age of 175, Abraham died and was buried in Machpelah next to his devoted and cherished wife, Sarah. Legend records that when Abraham died, so much was he loved and respected throughout the whole land that kings and princes came from great distances to pay him homage and to mourn for many days with his family.

Later, Isaac, too, was buried in the cave at Machpelah. Also, his son Jacob, who had gone down to Egypt to meet his son Joseph who had become great there, died in Egypt. Joseph, in a great procession, brought Jacob's body back to Hebron and buried it in the tomb with his fathers and mothers.

Hebron today, although in Israel, is a city with a large Arab population. It is located approximately 20 miles southwest of Jerusalem. The town's appearance presents evidence of its antiquity, and its atmosphere gives a feeling of the great historical role the city has played in religious history and in the lives of the patriarchs.

At Hebron one can visit the Moslem mosque believed to have been built over the cave of Machpelah. Beneath the center of this old mosque are the sepulchres which are pointed out as being the resting places of the remains of Abraham, Sarah, Isaac, Rebekah, Jacob, and Leah.

147

On the outskirts of Hebron is a gnarled and twisted old oak tree. This old tree is now covered with a tin roof and supported with wires and steel girders. It is pointed out as possibly being the tree under which Abraham pitched his tent.

Although these old shrines cannot be proved to be authentic, this land is the land of the patriarchs, and Hebron is a holy and sacred place both to the Hebrews and to the Moslems, who claim and revere Abraham as their ancestor. It is equally as sacred to the Christians.

Abraham, blessed of the Lord, was one of history's great characters. He was great because he loved and believed in the Lord, followed his commandments, loved and respected his neighbors and taught his children to do likewise. The Lord said of him:

"For I know him, that he will command his children and they shall keep the way of the Lord, to do justice and judgment; that the Lord may bring upon Abraham that which he hath spoken of him." (Gen. 18:19.)

An ancient oak tree near Hebron near where some believe Abraham pitched his tent.

Jericho

"the walls came tumbling down"

*". . . and it came to pass, when
the people heard the sound of the
trumpet, and the people shouted
with a great shout, that the wall
fell down flat, so that the people
went up into the city . . . "*
(Joshua 6:20.)

Excavation of the famous old walls of Jericho. The Mount of Temptation in the background.

Part of the main square in Jericho today.

JERICHO is believed to be the oldest city in Palestine and, according to legend, is one of the oldest cities in the world.

Archaeological excavations near the outskirts of the present city have been carried out at intervals over the more than 60 years.

Early excavations made at the site, known as "Tell el-Sultan," were by a German-Austrian expedition during 1907 to 1909. This group discovered two concentric rings of fortifications surrounding a ridge near the mountains to the northwest of Jericho. The outer ring of fortifications circled the hill with a six-foot brick wall about 25 feet high, with extremely thick foundations. Inside of this was another massive wall about 12 feet thick throughout. The leaders of this expedition, Ernst Sellin and Karl Watzinger, believed that the outer wall was destroyed about 1200 B.C.

In 1930, a British expedition made further investigations and found that the space between the two walls was filled with a considerable amount of rubble and that there were evidences of an extensively destructive fire. The leader of this expedition, John Garstang, dated the destruction of the inner wall at about 1400 B.C. Later, Father Hugues Vincent, Clarence Fisher and Alan Rowe independently signed statements with Garstang confirming his date of approximately 1400 B.C. One of the dating problems that all of these investigators faced, however, was the complete absence of pottery fragments in this stratum of the ruins. The shattered houses that had been along the walls of Jericho were empty. Apparently someone, somehow, had removed their contents, and this lack has made the dating more difficult.

One of the most amazing aspects of the Garstang excavation, however, was the discovery that the stones of the outer wall, when it was destroyed, had fallen outward and downhill but that the inner wall, nearer the crest of the hill, had fallen inward. Both of the walls showed evidence of violent destruction with large cracks and fissures.

As with other miraculous incidents described in the Bible, skeptics have attempted to explain away the story of the destruction of Jericho's walls, claiming that the incident probably never occurred. Archaeological research establishing the fact that the walls suffered a violent destruction, and also placing the time of the destruction at approximately the date when Joshua and the Children of Israel entered Palestine, should effectively answer these claims.

During the several excavations on the site, trenches have been dug straight down into bedrock. In the lower strata, evidences produced traces of habitation in the bronze age and, under that, in the stone age. Some of the excavated remains of Jericho's houses are judged to be over 7,000 years old.

As a result of a 1953 British expedition, Dr. Kathleen M. Kenyon claimed that Jericho probably was the oldest city in the world.

The best known biblical stories associated with Jericho are the Old Testament account of the destruction of the walls of the city during Joshua's conquest and the New Testament story of Jesus' parable of the Good Samaritan. Jericho is also remembered as the place where the prophets Elisha and Elijah were associated and where Elisha turned the bitter waters into sweet.

Every Bible student remembers the story of Joshua and Jericho's walls. After Moses' death, Joshua was instructed by the Lord to lead the Children of Israel into their Promised Land. Joshua immediately prepared the people to follow the Lord's instructions, but to enter the Promised Land, it was necessary to cross the Jordan River. Apparently, this was in the spring of the year, for the Jordan, which at this spot is near where it empties into the Dead Sea, was wide and deep and at flood stage. The Israelites had no boats or other fording facilities, but they faithfully followed their leader and the Jordan's waters were parted so that the whole company could pass through to the other side.

Two spies were then sent into the city and were given special help and protection by a woman named Rahab who lived in a house on the wall. Joshua also encountered a special messenger. From this messenger and from his two spies he learned that the inhabitants of the city stood in great fear of the Israelites, had no heart to fight, and the city was ripe for capture.

155

Following the Lord's instructions, Joshua marched his armies, his people and his priests, carrying the Ark of the Covenant, around the city for a week. Then, on the seventh day, at a pre-arranged signal, they all shouted and blew their horns in one great chorus. Jericho's walls came tumbling down.

According to biblical chronology, Joshua's conquest of Jericho took place approximately 1450 B.C. After the city fell, he instructed his people to gather up all of its gold, silver and valuable things that they might be burned as an offering to the Lord. Nothing was to be kept or used by the Israelites. Then a curse was put upon the city that whosoever should build it again should do so at the loss of both his oldest and his youngest sons.

After Joshua's days, a small village may have remained at the site of Jericho. However, the city was not rebuilt until some 500 years later when Heil the Bethelite did so, but only with the sacrifice of his oldest and his youngest sons.

During Elijah's and Elisha's time, a school of the prophets was established there. For their benefit, Elisha healed the bitter waters of the spring and made them sweet. Elisha's well, adjacent to the site of old Jericho, still flows fresh water for the use of the local inhabitants.

It will be recalled, according to the biblical account, that Elisha accompanied Elijah to Jericho, and it was at the Jordan near the city that Elijah

Elisha's well, near the walls of old Jericho where women still draw water.

the prophet ascended to heaven and that his mantle fell upon Elisha.

During Herod's reign, at the time of Jesus' ministry, a beautiful building complex was constructed about a mile east of the old site of Jericho. This apparently became one of Herod's winter capitals, and the ruins there, which, undoubtedly, have been added upon since his day, consist of palace courts, a hippodrome, a swimming pool and baths, fountains, gardens, and other imposing structures. This could have been the city which Jesus "was come nigh unto" when he healed the blind men. (Matt. 20:29, Mark 11:46, Luke 18:35.) Also, it could have been here that he met Zacchaeus, the wealthy tax collector who took him to his villa for dinner. (Luke 19:1.)

It was on the road from Jerusalem to Jericho that Jesus placed the story in his parable of the Good Samaritan. "A certain man went down from Jerusalem to Jericho, and fell among thieves." This was the story Jesus used to dramatize the answer to the question, "Who is my neighbor?" (Luke 10:30-37.)

During the past few years, Jericho has grown from a small village to a fairly sizable city. It lies approximately 1,250 feet below sea level, about six miles from the Dead Sea and near the shores of the Jordan. It is a warm tropical area and is becoming important agriculturally. From Jericho, today a new highway winds some 21 miles up the mountains to Jerusalem.

Remains of a beautiful palace once part of or built on the site of New Testament Jericho — Herod's magnificent Greco-Roman winter capital.

159

Joppa

"Jonah rose up to flee"

The port at old Joppa near where it is believed Jonah embarked on his fateful journey. Modern Tel Aviv in the background.

"But Jonah rose up to flee unto Tarshish from the presence of the Lord, and went down to Joppa; and he found a ship going to Tarshish: . . . " (Jonah 1:3.)

This old church is believed to have been built over the place where Peter received his vision of the sheet that descended from heaven.

162

NO OTHER city in the world has been so specially and peculiarly distinguished as Joppa. Twice throughout its long, eventful history, Joppa has been the place chosen by the Lord to emphasize to his prophets that his gospel is for all people and not exclusively for the Israelites or the Hebrews.

The remarkable incidents the Lord used to dramatize this fact are described herein. But, first, a few facts about this interesting city.

Joppa is another of the world's most ancient communities. Since antiquity it has been an important seaport gateway to Jerusalem. Joppa, Jaffa (Yafo) in Hebrew, is believed by some to have been derived from the Hebrew *yafe* (beautiful). More probably, however, it was named after Japheth, son of Noah, who, it is believed, founded the city soon after the flood.

The earliest reference to the city is found in Egyptian history of the eighteenth dynasty. Thutmose III, one of the Egyptian kings of this period, refers to Joppa as one of the tribute cities. It was during this era (1580-1085 B.C.) that Egypt colonized and ruled Palestine, Lebanon and the northern part of Syria.

Joppa was an important Mediterranean city during Solomon's times. When he was building the beautiful temple at Jerusalem, Joppa was used as a seaport through which building materials were brought to the city. King Hiram of Tyre, whose people were skilled in work in gold, silver, brass, iron, and particularly in wood, provided these materials to Solomon which were floated by sea to Joppa and from there carried up to Jerusalem. (2 Chronicles 2:16.)

When the Children of Israel entered their promised land, they could not conquer the fortified city of Joppa. Yet, the city was assigned to the Tribe of Dan. Later, the Maccabees conquered it from the Syrians, but it changed hands several times before the time of the life and ministry of Jesus Christ. Vespasian destroyed the city in A.D. 68. It was rebuilt and fought over many times during and after the time of the crusaders. Napoleon stormed and conquered it in 1799.

Joppa has also figured prominently in mythology. It was here, according to legend, that Andromeda was chained to a black rock in the harbor as a special offering to quiet the troubled sea for navigation. Perseus, riding on a winged horse, rescued Andromeda from a sea lion and then married her.

The dramatic incidents that emphasized the universality of the gospel were associated with Jonah and with the apostle Peter. It will be recalled that the prophet Jonah was instructed by the Lord to preach repentance to the wicked city of Nineveh.

Assyria, whose capital was Nineveh, was then just coming into power and was a serious threat to the security of the Israelites. Jonah had no desire to go into the camp of his enemies. Consequently, he sought escape by boarding a ship at Joppa which was sailing to Tarshish. As soon as the ship sailed, a great storm arose which threatened to destroy it. The sailors jettisoned the cargo, but when this measure failed they concluded that someone was aboard whose presence offended the gods. The sailors cast lots to determine who was guilty and the lot fell on Jonah, who was asleep below the deck. Jonah, aroused, immediately confessed that he was the source of the difficulty and instructed them to throw him overboard so that the storm would be quieted. This, at first, they refused to do, but the storm raged on. Reluctantly, they threw Jonah into the sea. Immediately the storm abated, and the seas became calm.

Jonah was swallowed by a great fish and remained in its stomach for three days and three nights before he was cast out, still alive, on the shore.

Jonah now had learned his lesson, and he went to Nineveh, where he warned the people that in 40 days the city would be destroyed. So forceful was his message that the city repented. Even the king was converted, and the Lord saved the city.

This angered Jonah, who had prophesied and hoped the enemies of his people would be destroyed. He built a hut on the outskirts of the city, where he sulked and prayed to the Lord that his life would be taken. He told the Lord that he knew all along that this would happen and he would be judged a false prophet. This, he said, was why he did not want to come to Nineveh in the first place.

165

The Lord caused a tree to grow over Jonah to give him shade; then, in one night, he allowed the tree to be destroyed. Jonah languished in the scorching sun and the hot winds praying that he would die. He was then reminded that if the Lord could raise a tree in a night and destroy it in a night, he could accept the repentance of the people in Nineveh. Moreover, all souls, even those in Nineveh, were precious in his sight and all deserved the blessing of his gospel.

During the early excavations at the site of Nineveh, in 1845, Layard discovered a large mound, some 100 feet high, which covered 40 acres. This mound was known by the natives as "Nebi Yunis" (the prophet Jonah), and they told of a legend that Jonah had preached repentance here and was buried in the mound. In fact, for a long time, no excavations were allowed on the mound because of the sanctity associated with the story and burial of the prophet Jonah.

The other dramatic incident at Joppa emphasizing the universality of the gospel was experienced by the apostle Peter. It will be recalled, according to the New Testament account, that the apostle was residing at Joppa, having just raised Tabitha from the dead, when Cornelius, a devout centurian at Caesarea, summoned Peter to come up from Joppa and preach the gospel to him and to his family and friends. Peter resisted because he thought that the gospel was to be preached only to the Jews.

It was then, at Joppa, that Peter had the remarkable vision in which a great sheet descended from heaven on which were all manner of four-footed beasts and other creeping, undesirable things. Peter was commanded to kill and eat these unfit things. From this manifestation, Peter also learned that the gospel was universal—for the Jews and gentiles alike.

Peter preached the gospel to Cornelius and his people and baptized them. The Holy Ghost then fell upon the whole group. This was the event which initiated the gentile Pentecost. (See Acts, chs. 9-10.)

In recent years, during the growth of Israel, the port of Joppa played an important role as a place through which thousands of refugees passed as they sought new homes in the new country. Today, the city is a suburb of Israel's largest city, Tel Aviv, and is the center of the country's rapidly developing fruit industry.

Megiddo

battlefield of the ages

Megiddo narrows through which historical armies have marched. Mount Tabor in the distance.

"Neither did Manasseh drive out . . . the inhabitants of Megiddo and her towns: but the Canaanites would dwell in that land." (Judges 1:27.)

An excavated Canaanite altar at Megiddo which probably dates back to the time of Abraham.

WHEN John the Revelator foresaw the last great battle of the world and called it Armageddon (Rev. 16:16), he must have had a clear knowledge of the tragic history of Megiddo. Har-Maged-don (Armageddon) means "the Mountain of Megiddo." Here, down through the ages, probably more important battles have been fought than at any other place in the world.

Megiddo actually is a fortress located on a hill at the mouth of the southwest passage which leads from the Plains of Sharon into the Plains of Jezreel (Esdraelon)—the largest valley in Israel. This valley is surrounded down to the coast of the Mediterranean by rugged hills including among their high places such famous biblical names as Mount Tabor, Mount Gilboa and Mount Carmel.

It was on Mount Tabor that, according to some authorities, Christ's transfiguration took place. Mount Gilboa is distinguished because it was on its slopes that Saul, first king of Israel, and his son Jonathan were killed in a battle with the Philistines.

Mount Carmel holds its place in biblical history because it was on its top that Elijah confounded the priests of Baal who were unable to entice their gods to function while the Almighty consumed Elijah's sacrifice in a ball of fire.

Due to the fact that the mountains at this point jut into the Mediterranean, the Plains of Jezreel and its narrow passage past the fortress of Megiddo into the Plains of Sharon provide the only easy access into the interior of Palestine and on south

171

into Egypt. This route was named in the Bible "Derekh Hayam"—the way of the sea. It also became an important Roman military artery known as "Via Maris."

Over this highway marched the great armies that came up the Mesopotamia Valley—up the Tigris and Euphrates rivers—and on down through the fertile crescent. All of these armies, unless they chose the sea route, were forced to move through this valley, up its narrow passage, and on past the fortress of Megiddo before they could continue their conquests into Palestine or into Egypt.

Battle after battle has been fought at Megiddo. Its earliest history records it as a Canaanite fortress. It was captured by Thutmose III in the twenty-third year of his reign (1478 B.C.). Even at that time its spoils were magnificent.

It was near the Waters of Megiddo that Deborah and Barak defeated the Canaanites under Sisera. In this battle the Hebrews were inferior in numbers and in power to the Canaanites whose soldiers were transported in armored chariots. Providentially, however, a great storm rose and flooded the River Kishon so that Sisera's chariots and his armies bogged down in the mud. Barak and Deborah then overpowered and conquered them.

Interestingly, it was on the banks of the Kishon that Elijah, after the demonstration of the Lord's power on Mount Carmel, had the 450 evil priests of Baal killed. This so enraged Jezebel, for whom they had worked, that she vowed to put Elijah to the same fate. She chased him through the Plains of Jezreel on through the Judean hills and 80 miles on down to Beersheba. Elijah, however, successfully eluded the angry woman.

Solomon, during his reign, depended heavily upon the fortifications at Megiddo. He restored and strengthened them and also used the fort as stables and housing for his 1,400 chariots and 12,000 horsemen. It was at Megiddo that Ahaziah, king of Judah, was killed. Here also the beloved King Josiah was slain in 610 B.C. when he attempted to interfere in a quarrel between the king of Assyria and the Egyptian Pharaoh Necho. His body was carried in a chariot from Megiddo to Jerusalem, where his death was mourned by all Israel.

The armies of Assyria, Babylonia, and Alexander the Great have all marched through the Plains of Esdraelon and have fought in and around Megiddo. It was also the scene of important battles during the crusader wars.

Even as late as the First World War, Megiddo played its important role. In 1918, British troops invaded the north of Palestine through the Megiddo Pass, and Field Marshal Allenby was given the title of Lord Allenby of Megiddo.

The first modern excavations were made at Megiddo in 1925 under the supervision of the Oriental Institute of the University of Chicago. Financed by John D. Rockefeller, Jr. and with the assistance of the Bible as a guide, the expedition uncovered fortifications dating back to 2,000 B.C.   **173**

Here was found the Seal of Shama, the servant of Jeroboam. Here also, standing approximately in the center of the vast ruins, is a restored Canaanite altar which was probably on the site when Abraham first made his way down through the Plains of Esdraelon and on into Shechem (Samaria) where he built his first altar and where the Lord promised him that all of the country of Canaan would be his for him and his family forever.

Today, the vast ramifications of the ruins of Megiddo overlook the beautiful Plains of Esdraelon and Jezreel which are undergoing an extensive and extremely productive agricultural development. With its plentiful water supply from the River Kishon and its tributaries, this is one of the more fertile plains in modern Israel.

The Plains of Esdraelon form a beautiful valley bordered on the west and south by Mount Carmel and the hills of Samaria, on the east by Mounts Gilboa and Tabor, and on the north and east by the hills of Nazareth and Galilee. The valley stretches down toward the sea to the plains of Acre and to the beautiful industrial city of Haifa on the Mediterranean.

As one walks among the ruins of Megiddo and views the impressive and peaceful valley below, it is only with difficulty that the imagination can visualize this area as the battlefield it has been throughout the ages and as the Armageddon that John the Revelator foresaw for it in the future.

174

A view of the Valley of Jezreel from Megiddo. Mount Tabor in the distance.

175

Nazareth

home of Mary, Joseph and Jesus

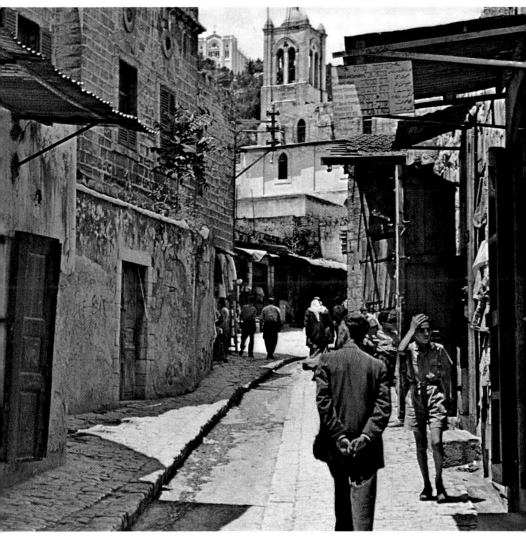

A street in Nazareth as it looks today. This old city has not changed much over the centuries.

"And he came and dwelt in the city called Nazareth: that it might be fulfilled which was spoken of by the prophets, He shall be called a Nazarene." (Matt. 2:23.)

Mary's well in Nazareth. This is the old well from which Jesus, Joseph, and Mary must have obtained their water.

NAZARETH is a small, rambling, unimpressive town nestled in the Galilean hills. Although it enjoys a place of renown in history, it is not significant now and, probably, was considered an unimportant town during the time when Jesus lived there.

There is no reference to Nazareth in the Old Testament. A reference in the New Testament indicates that the town was not too well thought of.

It will be recalled, according to the Gospel of John, that Jesus was selecting his disciples and had already chosen Simon Peter, his brother Andrew and Philip. Philip, apparently, was acquainted with Nathanael, who was a good man, and he told Nathanael that they had found the leader of whom Moses and the prophets had written. He was, Philip said, Jesus of Nazareth, the son of Joseph. Nathanael then said to him, "Can there any good thing come out of Nazareth?" (John 1:46.) Nathanael was not well impressed with Nazareth, but when he met Jesus, he immediately knew he was the Son of God and the King of Israel. (John 1:49.)

During the time when Jesus was growing up in Nazareth, this town was a typical, small, quaint Jewish village. Perhaps, much as the old city is today, its houses and buildings were scattered over several small hills with its narrow streets winding up and down the hills and through the several ravines or valleys over which the town is situated.

Due to the nature of the rock strata in the Galilean hills, there are numerous caves in and around

179

Nazareth and, possibly, many of these, during the lifetime of Jesus, were inhabited. In fact, some scholars believe Joseph and Mary's home was in one of these caves, or grottos.

Owing to the fact that Nazareth, during Jesus' time, was situated on the main trade route which ran from Damascus, through Philadelphia, Jerash and the Galilean cities to the Mediterranean coast at Acre, it is quite likely that Nazareth, although small, was a busy, cosmopolitan place. These Roman trade routes were important arteries and were guarded carefully by Roman soldiers who, it is believed, maintained a garrison at Nazareth.

Approximately in the center of Nazareth is the town square. On one side of the square is an old well which is pointed out as being the well from which Mary, Joseph and Jesus may have drawn their water. In view of the fact that this is the only well in the immediate vicinity, it is quite likely that this is true. In fact, the "Grotto" in which Mary and Joseph are believed to have made their home is only a short distance from this old well.

In Nazareth, Joseph worked as a carpenter and trained Jesus in this trade. Carpentry work, in those days, was quite different from what it is today. Nazareth houses, then and now, were made largely of limestone or adobe, were covered with a flat roof made of poles, branches and thick clay and usually contained no windows. There was little carpentry work connected with the building trades and, consequently, this skill most probably consisted mainly in making wooden tools, plows, yokes and, possibly, some household furniture.

During Jesus' time there were no manufacturing establishments nor lumber yards. Joseph and Jesus, in applying their trade, likely obtained their wood from trees in the surrounding hills and worked and shaped the lumber into the finished items which they produced.

Nazareth, with its cosmopolitan atmosphere, its military and travel activities and its variety of languages, Greek, Roman, Aramaic and Hebrew—would have been an interesting place for a young man to grow into manhood. Under the wise guidance and supervision of his parents, Jesus would have learned much about the world and about human nature in this old town.

Although small and relatively unimportant among even the cities in Palestine, Nazareth played its significantly important role during the early life of Jesus. It was here that the angel Gabriel came to announce the coming birth of the Christ. After their flight into Egypt to avoid Herod's wrath, Mary, Joseph and Jesus came back to Nazareth. And here the Lord grew up "in wisdom and stature, and in favor with God and man." (Luke 2:52.)

At the beginning of his ministry, Jesus preached one of his first sermons in a synagogue in Nazareth. It was on this occasion when he claimed he was fulfilling a prophecy made by Esaias that his townspeople became angry with him and took him to a precipice nearby and attempted to throw him over it. "But he passing through the midst of them went his way" and came to Capernaum, a few miles away, where he established his Galilean headquarters.

After Jesus' ministry, Nazareth sank again into obscurity. In Hebrew literature, the earliest reference to the town was made by the poet Eliezer Kalir, in about the seventh century. In his elegy on the destruction of Jerusalem, this writer mentioned a family of priests who resided in Nazareth. Another early comment about the city was made by a Christian pilgrim who visited Nazareth in A.D. 570. He wrote, "The charm of the Hebrew women of this city is greater than those of the entire land."

Today, in a Hebrew country, the majority of Nazareth's inhabitants are Christians and Arabs. The town is still small and quaint, probably not too much changed from what it was some 2,000 years ago.

A general view of Nazareth as it looks today.

Nazareth

recent biblical excavations

A garden in Nazareth near which is the grotto where Joseph, Mary and Jesus may have lived.

"And Nathanael said unto him, Can there any good thing come out of Nazareth? Philip saith unto him, Come and see." (John 1:46.)

TERRA SANTA MONASTERY IN NAZARETH.
Built on top of the site where Jesus may have lived.

ALTHOUGH Nazareth, particularly to the Christians, is full of Bible history, there are four biblical sites that are most significant. One of these, as indicated above, is the shrine known as Mary's Well, from which the family would have drawn water. The others are three sites that have been archaeologically excavated. The place where Jesus, Joseph, and Mary are believed to have lived is in a "*grotto*," which is below the surface and which can be visited. Over this grotto the Terra Santa Monastery has been constructed, the surrounding area of which displays a number of interesting artifacts uncovered during the excavation.

An excavation has also been recently completed at the Church of the Annunciation, believed to have been built over the place where Gabriel, the angel, visited Mary to tell her that she would be the mother of Jesus. Another of these excavations is at the Church of St. Joseph, believed to have been built over the place where Joseph lived.

Baptismal Fonts in These Churches

Some of the interesting features uncovered in the excavations at both of these churches are the baptismal fonts. Friar B. Bagatti, of the Studium Biblicum Franciscanum, who supervised these excavations and who prepared a report, *Excavations in Nazareth*, vol. 1, has indicated in his report that both of these basins, in the two churches, undoubtedly were baptismal fonts. In excavating

under the mosaic of the central knave of the Shrine
of the Annunciation, workers uncovered a basin full
of big stones, earth, and many objects of pottery.
First impressions upon seeing the basin were that
it was the ordinary installation for a wine or olive
press. Friar Bagatti writes, however, that "a more
careful examination led us to abandon that idea in
favor of a place used for baptisms. There are three
principle reasons for our change of mind; first, the
shape of the basin itself in relation to the size;
second, the Graffiti [religious drawings] in the plas-
ter covering the wall; third, comparison with a like
basin existing under St. Joseph's Church."[1]

Friar Bagatti's report continues in its description
of the basin (font) with the decorations in the plas-
ter on the walls and the mosaic on the floor. He
also found seven steps leading into the font.

In the excavations at the site of the Church of
St. Joseph, as already indicated, another basin, or
font, was uncovered. It also had a "stairway of
seven steps carved out of the rock on the south side
[which gave] access from the pavement down to
the bottom of the basin. The pavement of the area
that enclosed the basin is, like the stairway and the
basin, covered with mosaic, although only bits of it
have remained."[2]

Both of the fonts contained sculptured depressions in a corner, which the archaeologists called
vases. These depressions are somewhat of a mystery
to the archaeologists in that they were fully sculp-

tured and lined also with mosaic. As we studied the report we could not help but wonder if they may not have been receptacles for heated stones which, for baptismal purposes, would have taken the chill from the water. Stones which could have been used for this purpose were discovered in the excavation.

The Antiquity of Baptism

Most Christian churches teach that baptism is essentially a Christian rite which dates from the time of John the Baptist. This belief persists in spite of the fact that there is plentiful evidence that baptism by immersion has been a sacred religious rite down through the ages.[3] John, of course, was preaching repentance and baptizing in the wilderness of Judea *before* Jesus was baptized by him. The fact that John was baptizing aroused no particular excitement. Had it not been for the fact that he baptized Jesus, it is doubtful that religious historians of the time would have paid much attention to his baptism. In other words, baptism was an accepted religious principle which had been practiced long before the time even of John the Baptist. The Essenes, or Dead Sea covenanters, were baptizing by immersion long before the time of Jesus.

Although the Old Testament makes no direct reference to baptism, the Hebrew Talmud is unmistakably clear that "proselytes of righteousness" were required to accept baptism prior to admission into

189

the church. Dr. Alfred Edersheim says, "All writers are agreed that three things were required for the admission of such proselytes: circumcision, baptism and sacrifice." He further states, "The fact that baptism was absolutely necessary to make a proselyte, is so frequently stated [in the Talmud] as not to be disputed."[4]

Dr. Edersheim draws an interesting parallel between the missions of John the Baptist and Elijah the prophet. He claims that John's baptism was the counterpart of "Elijah's novel rite on Mt. Carmel," when the priests of Baal were confounded.[5]

Scholars of the Talmud and the Old Testament scriptures see evidence that baptism might have been practiced by Abraham when he and his family left their homeland together with "the souls that they had gotten in Haran."[6] These souls, according to Dr. Adam Clarke, were actually proselytes, or converts. If these souls were proselytes, they must have been baptized. Hebrew scholars are agreed that no proselyte came into the Hebrew religion without baptism.[7] It is interesting to note that The Church of Jesus Christ of Latter-day Saints teaches this antiquity of baptism as an essential part of the plan of salvation. The Pearl of Great Price, one of the standard scriptures of the Church, plainly states that Adam was baptized and that he taught this principle to his children, who, in turn, taught it to their children.

190 The prophet Enoch practiced and taught bap-

tism. Noah also knew of the importance of this ordinance and taught it to his children and to the people of his day.

In two books of the Old Testament, Solomon describes the temple he constructed in Jerusalem and gives details of the "baptismal font" built in the temple which he calls a sea.[8] The "baptismal font," which Solomon says was used by the priests for "washings," was made of brass and laid on the backs of 12 oxen, three of whose heads pointed outward in all four directions.

Mode of Baptism

The discovery of these old baptismal fonts in Nazareth brings new proof, not only of the correct mode of baptism, immersion, but also of the importance of it as an essential part of the plan of salvation. The fact that these old churches had baptismal fonts constructed as a fundamental part of their architecture provides strong evidence of the fact that baptism was essential to entry into their church and, in the minds of their church leaders, essential to salvation. Christian writers connected with the early primitive church had a clear understanding of the correct form of baptism. For example, Tertullian wrote that it made no difference where or in what water baptism was performed so long as "we are immersed in water." Justin Martyr wrote, "In the name of the Father, and of Jesus Christ, and of the Holy Ghost, the immersion in water is performed."[9]

Originally, the mode of baptism was immersion. In fact, the word itself, baptism, means to immerse. Jesus set the pattern when he himself was baptized by immersion by John. He said that he did this to "fulfill all righteousness."

Why other modes of baptism, such as sprinkling and pouring, were introduced into religious procedures must be incomprehensible to any serious student of the scriptures. Evidently, these other modes were introduced as compromises and as a result of loss of authority and due to apostasy from the true principles of the gospel as given by the Savior during his ministry.

After his crucifixion, Jesus instructed his disciples to "go ye therefore, and teach all nations, baptizing them in the name of the Father, and of the Son, and of the Holy Ghost." Surely he meant that they should baptize by immersion and with the authority which he alone could give to them.

———

[1]B. Bagatti, *Excavations in Nazareth,* vol. 1 (Franciscan Printing Press, 1969), pp. 116-23.

[2]Ibid., pp. 228-32.

[3]See Henry F. Brown, *Baptism Through the Centuries* (Mountain View, California: Pacific Press Association, 1965).

[4]Alfred Edersheim, *The Life and Times of Jesus the Messiah* (Grand Rapids, Michigan: W. B. Erdmans Publishing Company, 1956), vol. 2, p. 745.

[5]Ibid., vol. 1, p. 255. See also 1 Kings 18:25-39.

[6]Genesis 12:5.

[7]Adam Clarke, *Commentary on the Holy Bible* (New York: Layne and Sanford, 1843), vol. 1, p. 92.

[8]See 1 Kings 7:23; 2 Chron. 4:2-5.

[9]See James E. Talmage, *The Great Apostasy* (Salt Lake City: The Church of Jesus Christ of Latter-day Saints, 1965), p. 93.

Basin excavated under Church of the Annunciation believed to have been a baptismal font.

The Qumran
Community

discovery of the Dead Sea Scrolls

The caves at Qumran from which some of the Dead Sea Scrolls were taken.

"Now the acts of David the king,
first and last, behold, they are
written in the book of Samuel
the seer, and in the book of
Nathan the prophet, and in the
book of Gad the seer . . ."
(1 Chron. 29:29.)

Baptismal Font at the Qumran Community.

WHEN, in the spring of 1947, the young Moslem boy, Muhammad "The Wolf," accidentally found old records in the Dead Sea caves, he had no way of knowing either the importance of his discovery or the religious controversy it would generate.

The story of the Dead Sea Scrolls is now well known. Briefly, a group of Bedouin contrabanders, in the spring of 1947, were camped near an ancient spring, Ain Feshka, near the Qumran Wadi at the northwest corner of the Dead Sea. The party apparently was engaged in the illegal business of attempting to smuggle goods from Jordan into Palestine without paying the established custom duties.

While they were thus encamped, one of the youths of the group, Muhammad Odh-dhib, was looking for a lost goat in one of the many caves that interlace the limestone hills in the area. While making this search, he accidentally found some old earthen jars in which were some linen-wrapped, parchment scrolls. These old records, and others later found in this and other caves in the vicinity, proved to be a part of an ancient library apparently hidden there by a people who lived in the vicinity prior to, during, and shortly after the birth and ministry of Jesus Christ.

Later, archaeological investigations in the area uncovered the remains of an ancient community in which, at one time, several thousand people lived, worked, and performed their religious ceremonies.

The records discovered in the caves proved to

be of three different types. There were parts or complete texts of several books which are contained in the Old Testament. There were several records, maintained by the people themselves, which contained some of their own history, an outline of the organization of their community and a description of some of their religious beliefs. In addition, there were also portions of records of other "scriptures," some of which have been known to a few scholars, but which never were a part of the canon of either the Old or the New Testaments.

Soon after the original discovery, scholars cautiously began to predict that these old records might prove to be of great archaeological and religious importance. Now, after a quarter of a century since the first scrolls were deciphered and translated, it is generally agreed that this discovery of ancient records is without doubt the most important ever made in Palestine and probably the most significant made anywhere at any time.

One of the reasons why the discovery of these old records is proving to be even more important than any scholar's wildest dreams is that the scrolls provide scientific historical information covering the period of man's history, a most critical period, about which very little has been known. This is the span of approximately 250 years from about 150 B.C. to A.D. 100. This was the period into which came the life of Jesus and his forerunners and disciples. This was the time which scholars

The ruins at Qumran with one of the baptismal fonts in the foreground.

believe saw the origins of Christianity and the foundation era on which Christian churches base their beginnings.

Yet, unfortunately, until the discovery of ancient records in the caves near the Dead Sea, this was basically a period of literary silence. No authentic records were available which dated from this time. All that is known about this period comes to us from writings of a much later date which purport to cover historical and religious events which took place during this period.[1]

Moreover, as additional information has become available from the deciphering and translation of these old records, a number of significant previously widely held concepts about religious history have faced the necessity of revision. Among these are the conclusions that every textbook previously written about this period of religious history now needs to be revised. Many theories about the origins of New Testament writings are now in question or out of date. Previously held conclusions regarding the sources and origin of certain Old Testament books now need to be restudied. The controversy regarding the relative authenticity of the Septuagint as compared with the Massoretic texts must be reopened. Previously settled conclusions regarding Christian origins need to be reconsidered. The

[1]See J. T. Malik, "Dix Ans de decouvertes dans le desert de Judah," Paris, 1957. J. N. Allegro, *The Dead Sea Scrolls* (Baltimore, 1957), pp. 13, 36. G. Frederick Owen, *Archaeology of the Bible* (New York: Revell Company, 1961), p. 347.

question of "who were the Essenes?" is given a new answer, and the questions of to whom and by whom certain New Testament books were written may now need new study.

Josephus, Pliny, and Philo, ancient historians who lived during or near the beginning of the Christian era, wrote about the Essenes. They described them as a peculiarly interesting group of people who lived near the shores of the Dead Sea and who may have had other communities throughout the Palestinian area. There is no doubt now that the Dead Sea Scrolls were the records used and preserved by this people.

Who Were the Essenes?

An interesting and enlightening treatise has recently been published which connects the "Essenes," or "Dead Sea Covenanters," at least partially with the "Hebrews" to whom an epistle was written in the New Testament. This treatise[2] presents the interesting thesis that perhaps the Essenes were the Hebrews or, at least, were a group of the Essenes who had joined the Christian Church and, after Christ's crucifixion, had begun gradually to drift back into their previous beliefs. The epistle to them, the book of Hebrews, was written by one of the Christian church leaders who may have tried

---

[2]Yagael Yadin, "Scripta Hierosolymitana," *The Dead Sea Scrolls and the Epistle to the Hebrews,* Hebrew University, p. 36.

through his letter to persuade this group that the Christian gospel they had accepted was the true gospel and that they should discard their old beliefs and hold fast to their new covenants. Although this thesis has yet to be proved, the evidence presented in the research is persuasive.

The Qumran Community is located on a plateau overlooking the Dead Sea approximately six miles from the Jordanian resort area on the sea near Jericho. The ruins, now almost completely excavated, show evidence of extensive community life made possible through an ingenious system of canals which caught the scanty rainfall and conserved it for use throughout the long dry periods.

The Qumran Community is one of the most interesting of the Palestinian area's many impressive and fantastic archaeological wonders. As the story and importance of the Dead Sea Scrolls discovery becomes more widely known and as additional facts about this ancient people come to light, this archaeological excavation is sure to become an important center of worldwide religious interest.[3]

----

[3]See O. P. Robinson, *The Dead Sea Scrolls and Original Christianity* (Salt Lake City: Deseret Book Co., 1958), and *The Challenge of the Scrolls — How Old Is Christ's Gospel?* (Salt Lake City: Deseret Book Co., 1965).

Excavations of the Qumran Community with Dead Sea in the background.

Sebaste

ancient city of Samaria

Joseph's tomb at Shechem near old Sebaste.

"And Israel said unto Joseph, Do not thy brethren feed the flock in Shechem? Come, and I will send thee unto them. . . . " (Gen. 37:13.)

Jacob's well near Nablus and Sebaste. The priest in the background is the custodian of this ancient well.

HEN Abraham and his party left Haran and entered the Land of Canaan, his first stop was at Shechem, in the Valley of Samaria. Here, he built an altar and gave thanks to the Lord for the blessings he had received and for the promises the Lord had given that he and his family would possess this good land. Later the whole area was given by Abraham to Jacob who dug a well here and established temporary residence. Jacob then gave the land as an inheritance to his son, Joseph.

From the time of Abraham's first entry into the Samaritan Valley, this territory has played a significant role in Israel's history. It was here that many important Old Testament battles took place and that the final scattering of Israel occurred.

This historical event transpired at approximately B.C. 724 when the Assyrian king Sargon finally succeeded in his siege of Samaria and conquered the fortified community. To make sure that the Jews would no longer be troublesome to them, the Assyrians deported all of Samaria's leading inhabitants and scattered them throughout the Assyrian kingdom. They replaced these people with immigrants selected from other places—people who they believed would not assist nor cooperate with the Israelites.

Later, because these "strangers" found it difficult to become integrated into the area, a selected number of Israelite priests were returned to Samaria. From these and from the intermixing of the settlers Sargon had brought into the area, eventually the Samaritan people evolved.

As the Samaritans grew in strength and prominence, they became a serious source of irritation to the Jews. During Jesus' time, these two peoples were extremely antagonistic and would tolerate no traffic or association with each other. Orthodox Jews, in fact, would not even travel through Samaritan country. This is the reason why some of Christ's disciples were surprised and critical of him when he took the road through Samaria during his ministry. It was on one of these trips when Jesus met the Samaritan woman at Jacob's Well and, in return for a drink of the well's water, offered her "living water," saying, . . . "whosoever drinketh of the water that I shall give him shall never thirst." (John 4:14.)

During Herod's administration in Palestine, he was given supervision over Judea, Samaria and Galilee. Being a crafty and a scheming politician, Herod immediately set to work to please and impress the Roman emperor, Tiberius Caesar Augustus.

Herod built impressive cities throughout Palestine and named them after the emperor. Caesarea was constructed on the Mediterranean coast, and a beautiful temple was built there for the emperor. Tiberias was established on the shores of Galilee and became a favorite resort area. Herod then built a magnificent city on the top of the Samaritan hills which he called Sebaste. Sebastos is the Greek word for Augustus and Augustus means "worthy of reverence." Thus, with the construction of Sebaste, Herod had completed his triad of costly and imposing monuments to his emperor.

208   It is not known to what extent Caesar might have

Ruins at Sebaste believed by some to be where John the Baptist was in prison before his beheading.

enjoyed these cities, or, for that matter, whether or not he ever visited them. With their construction, however, Herod had accomplished his task, and he justified his extravagant endeavor on the grounds of doing honor to the emperor.

After Herod's time, Sebaste had a checkered history of conquest, destruction and reconstruction. Early in the Christian era Sebaste was invaded by the Roman Emperor Vespasian, who inflicted a crushing blow upon the Samaritans. Later, the city was conquered and destroyed both by the Moslems and the crusaders.

Today, extensive ruins of Sebaste and ancient Samaria exist about 15 miles northwest of the modern city of Nablus. These ruins give evidence of the one-time existence of substantial fortifications and impressive buildings.

The ruins cover the top of a hill in Israeli territory looking down into the Valley of Samaria and out over the hills and plains of Palestine. At the foot of the hill is an old chariot road which, in all probability, carried the horse-drawn traffic which Herod brought into the area. To the west is the Valley of Dothan where, it is claimed, Joseph's brothers kept their flocks and where they connived among themselves to dispose of him by selling him to a caravan on its way to Egypt.

To the east of the hill and up the valley beyond Nablus is Jospeh's tomb. Here, only a short distance from Jacob's Well, is the place, it is claimed, where Joseph's bones were buried after they were brought up from Egypt.

Valley at Samaria where Jacob's sons may have pastured their flocks. Old Roman aqueduct in center.

Sodom
and Gomorrah

those wicked cities

*"And Lot lifted up his eyes, and
beheld all the plain of Jordan,
that it was well watered every
where, before the Lord destroyed
Sodom and Gomorrah, even as
the garden of the Lord . . . "*
(Gen. 13:10.)

The Jordan River at or near the place where Jesus was baptized, a few miles from where the river empties into the Dead Sea and in the vicinity, some believe, of the ancient sites of Sodom and Gomorrah.

A salt formation at Sedom near the Dead Sea not far from the possible site of ancient Sodom.

(*Photo Courtesy of Israel Government Tourist Office.*)

SODOM and Gomorrah, and the three other cities of the Plains of the Dead Sea, were, according to the scriptures, the most wicked cities in the world. So degradingly corrupt and evil were the people of these cities that the Lord determined they must be destroyed.

How the Lord rained fire and brimstone upon these cities is one of the better known stories in the scriptures.

It will be recalled that Abraham was sitting before his tent at Hebron, when angels appeared. Among other things, they told him if the people in the cities of Sodom and Gomorrah were as wicked as the cries against them coming up to heaven had indicated, they would be destroyed. Possibly because his nephew Lot and his family were living in Sodom, Abraham argued with the angels, asking if they would destroy the righteous with the wicked. If he could find fifty righteous in the city, would they spare the place? The angels replied that they would spare the city for the sake of fifty righteous. Then Abraham bargained until he obtained agreement that if even ten righteous were found in the city it would not be destroyed. But ten righteous souls could not be found—only Lot, his wife, and his two daughters.

Consequently, the Lord determined to destroy the city and, after Lot and his family were removed, caused fire and brimstone to come down upon it and upon Gomorrah and two of the other five wicked cities. The little city of Zoar was spared because

Lot and his two daughters sought refuge there. Unfortunately, Lot's wife, disobedient to the angels' instructions, turned to look back at the destruction and was changed into a pillar of salt.

Apocryphal books of the scriptures describe some of the sins of the inhabitants of these plains cities and they were evil beyond description. Even strangers who happened to wander through the city gates were killed or cruelly tormented. This is probably why, when the two angels came into the city and were invited by Lot into his home, the people surrounded the house and tried forcibly to take them. When Lot resisted, the Sodomites threatened him and only when the angels blinded them were their efforts thwarted. One of the important reasons why the people were so wicked was because their judges and rulers were exceedingly evil.

Considerable disagreement exists regarding the possible location of Sodom and Gomorrah. Some Bible scholars believe these wicked cities were situated near the south end of the Dead Sea. In fact, sites now known as Sedom and Amora, located near the southern end of the Dead Sea, are pointed out as being the authentic locations of these cities. Even a geological formation located in the mountains there, which resembles the form of a standing woman, is pointed out as being the salt pillar of Lot's wife. A cave in the hills is known as the Sedom cave. Presently, a youth hostel is located there. These sites are located in Israel territory near the Jordanian border.

On the other hand, many Bible scholars, including both Hebrew and Arab historians, maintain that the plains cities were in the Jordan Valley at the north end of the Dead Sea where the river empties into the sea. This location is based primarily upon the authority of Genesis 13, which states that after Lot and Abraham separated, Lot chose the Plain of Jordan and "dwelled in the cities of the plain, and pitched his tent toward Sodom." (Gen. 13:12.) This passage would seem to place the location near the northern end of the Dead Sea. Nevertheless, there is sufficient evidence on both sides of the question to justify consideration of both locations.

Again, as with so many of the ancient biblical sites, the specific location may be in doubt, but the area around the Dead Sea is the authentic place where these dramatic events occurred. Visitors who have the time will find it most interesting to arrange to visit both areas and, thereby, can be reasonably sure that they have walked over the ground which Abraham knew so well and where Lot and his daughters escaped the fire and brimstone showered upon the scriptures' most wicked cities.

Solomon's Mines

the Bible guides their discovery

Authors at the Red Sea. Edom Mountains in the background.

"But as for you, turn you, and take your journey into the wilderness by the way of the Red sea." (Deut. 1:40.)

Solomon's pillars near the Red Sea and near the location of Solomon's mines.

WHEN, after 40 years of wandering in the desert, Moses and the Children of Israel looked across the Jordan, they saw "a good land, a land of brooks of water, of fountains and depths that spring out of valleys and hills; A land of wheat, and barley, and vines, and fig trees, and pomegranates; a land of oil, olive, and honey; . . . a land whose stones are iron, and out of whose hills thou mayest dig brass." (Deut. 8:7-9.)

Although Moses saw this bounteous land and knew of its great potentialities, due to the stiff-necked stubbornness and wickedness of the people he had brought out of bondage in Egypt, and had guided through 40 years of wilderness wanderings, Moses himself was not permitted to enter into this Promised Land. Yet, he clearly foresaw its future.

Through the Lord's divine instructions, Moses knew that Joshua would lead the victorious Israelite armies throughout the entire territory which had been promised to their fathers Abraham, Issac, and Jacob. Following Joshua's time the Israelite victories would gradually be consolidated until the whole area from the Red Sea on the south to the Great Sea on the north and from Egypt to the Euphrates would be theirs as one rich Promised Land.

This conquest and consolidation, however, did not take place for some 435 years when, under the inspired leadership of David, the whole land was conquered and made secure.

Following David's great victories, Solomon, his son, made effective peace treaties with his neighbors and devoted his energies and wisdom to building the kingdom to its all-time zenith of power and glory. Solomon had asked the Lord to grant him "an understanding heart." Because he had made this humble request the Lord not only gave him wisdom and understanding but also, "both riches, and honour: so that there shall not be any among the kings like unto thee all thy days." (I Kings 3:13.)

Solomon strengthened, fortified, and beautified the cities throughout the land of Israel and built the beautiful temple on Mount Moriah in Jerusalem. This magnificent edifice he garnished with gold and carvings.

With the help of his friend, Hiram, from Tyre and with the skilled workmanship and materials from the Sidonians, Solomon built beautiful structures throughout Israel and spread the fame of the glory of his kingdom into the neighboring world. Kings and princes from the surrounding areas heard of Solomon's great wisdom and accomplishments and came to him for advice and consultation. Even the distant Queen of Sheba came up through the Red Sea with her caravans of servants and costly presents to visit and pay homage to Solomon. The wisdom, pomp, wealth, and glory which he displayed to her so impressed her that she went away marveling.

Some of Solomon's great wealth was imported from surrounding countries. Much of it, however, he developed from natural resources in his own country. The scriptures and ancient historical records indicate, for example, that among other things, he had extensive and productive copper mines in the mountains not many miles north of the Red Sea. So vast and productive were these copper developments that he maintained thousands of workers, possibly slaves, digging, smelting and refining the metal.

Although biblical and historical records testified of the fact that Solomon had developed these mines, it was not until after the creation of the state of Israel, in 1948, that serious exploration was undertaken to locate and develop this mineral. A few years previously, however, in 1939-1940, a scientific expedition led by the archaeologist, Nelson Glueck, found the remains of a big copper smelting and refining plant not far from what is now the town of Eilat on the Red Sea. Using the Bible and other old historical records as guides, Mr. Glueck and subsequent explorers discovered these old ruins on the top of a rocky hill about 17 miles north of Eilat and not far from the Pillars of Solomon. The archaeological remains consist of a watchtower, which probably guarded the prisoners or workers, a series of smelting pits and the apparent remains of a smelting plant.

Using these old relics as guides, in succeeding years, Israeli geologists located in the vicinity rich copper deposits near which now has been constructed a modern copper refinery. During 1959-60, the first year of full operations, from 435,000 tons of copper ore mined in the vicinity, this refinery produced copper cement containing 5,400 tons of 100

223

per cent metallic copper.

By the end of this first year, exports to Britain, Brazil, Germany, Japan, and Portugal earned for the installation approximately four and one-half million dollars which made the refinery, during its first year, a profitable venture. Since that time, operations have been accelerated with the objective of doubling the output of the plant. Geological tests in this area, obviously the old site of Solomon's mines, have established that there are proved ore reserves here totaling approximately 19 million tons and total estimated reserves in the neighborhood of from 30 to 35 million tons.

Under the effective incentive of national need and with the encouragement of scriptural records which indicate the existence not only of copper but also of iron and other valuable metals, modern Israel is currently engaged in a series of scientific exploration projects which will, in all probability, discover and develop additional strategic resources upon which the new nation can build a strong economy.

Already, considerable industrialization is developing in Israel with significant production of potash, bromine, phosphates and other fertilizers. Although Israel is small and arid and, compared with some of its more economically fortunate neighbors, relatively poor, it is both fascinating and impressive to observe its rapid economic development.

With determined human effort, with the help of the Bible as a guide, and with faith and vision exemplified by Moses, this little country is beginning to "blossom as the rose" and may yet be a land "flowing with milk and honey."

The general area of Solomon's mines near the Red Sea.

Tiberias

one of Herod's playgrounds

The Sea of Galilee with ruins of old Roman fort in the foreground. Mount Hermon in Syria in background.

"Howbeit there came other boats from Tiberias nigh unto the place where they did eat bread." (John 6:23.)

Fishermen on the Sea of Galilee near where Jesus selected some of his disciples.

TIBERIAS, during the period of the ministry of Jesus, was a Gentile city in the center of an important Hebrew area. Although it was near where Jesus lived, there is no record in the scriptures that he ever taught there or, for that matter, ever visited the city. In fact, the only biblical reference to the city of Tiberias is in the Gospel according to John which records that boats had come from there. (John 6:23.) John makes other references to Tiberias, but when he does so he refers to the lake itself, which the Romans had named Tiberias after the city.

The town of Tiberias was built by Herod (A.D. 16-22) who established it primarily as a recreational and resort area.

Although summers at Tiberias are hot, the average temperature year-around is pleasant and attractive. The lake itself is approximately 685 feet below sea level and, consequently, gets very little cold weather during the winter. Moreover, one of the finest hot springs in the Middle East is located at the site of ancient Tiberias, and it was around these baths that Herod constructed his city. Herod and his Roman friends undoubtedly thoroughly enjoyed their frequent sorties into this attractive area where they had the fresh water recreational opportunities of the beautiful Sea of Galilee plus the possible therapeutic benefits of the hot springs.

Tiberias, however, was apparently thoughtlessly built by Herod on the remains of an ancient graveyard. This circumstance made the city an unclean place for the Jews, and Herod had difficulty in forcing the people to inhabit it. This may have been one reason why no scriptural reference exists indicating that Jesus visited it.

However, like Caesarea, Tiberias was a Roman city named after the emperor, and it embodied many pagan characteristics distasteful to the Jews. This fact also may have influenced Jesus and caused him to give it a wide berth during his ministry.

Nevertheless, after the fall of Jerusalem an almost complete reversal took place in the Jewish attitude toward the city. During the early Christian period it became the center of rabbinic teaching. Judah, The Holy, editor of the Jewish Mishna, lived and worked here and produced the Mishna in about A.D. 200. Also, the Jewish scholars who compiled the first Jerusalem Talmud, about A.D. 400, did their work here. The tombs of other prominent early Jewish leaders are in the neighborhood.

Although Constantine built a beautiful church here and established one of the early Christian bishoprics, with its Hebrew emphasis, Tiberias never became an important center of Christianity. The city was seized by the Arabs in A.D. 637, and later was conquered by the crusaders and then lost by them to Saladin in 1187. In 1837 it was almost completely destroyed by an earthquake.

The Jordan River as it leaves the Sea of Galilee near Tiberias.

Today, as in ancient times, Tiberias is again an important and growing city—the capital of Galilee. Not only is it the center of a significant agricultural area, it also is an extremely attractive recreation and tourist spot.

Located on the shores of Galilee and stretching back up the mount to its rear, the city commands a magnificent view across the beautiful blue lake and on to the towering peak of Mount Hermon across the border in Syria. Mount Hermon, whose elevation reaches nearly 10,000 feet, is snow-capped much of the year and, consequently, presents a dominant view across the lake to the inhabitants of Tiberias.

Despite its original repugnance to the Jews, long before the creation of the modern State of Israel, Tiberias had become an important Jewish center. Since 1948, however, it has enjoyed a rapid growth and has become a choice center which attracts visitors from all over the world.

Sea of Galilee with snow covered Mount Hermon in background.

Tsefat

Israel's city of mysticism

A street scene in the old city of Tsefat as it looks today.

"For, behold, I have made thee
this day a defenced city, and an
iron pillar, and brasen walls
against the whole land . . ."
(Jer. 1:18.)

A general view of Tsefat in the Galilean hills.
(Photo Courtesy of Israel Government Tourist Office.)

SEFAT (Safed—in Arabic) is one of the most picturesque towns in modern Israel. The town is situated in the tops of the rugged mountains north and slightly west of the Sea of Galilee. It is the northernmost city in Israel and is the capital of Upper Galilee. The tops of the town's surrounding hills provide a spectacular view of the Sea of Galilee in the distance, of the small valley which once contained the water of Little Lake Hula and the deep gorge through which the Jordan drops rapidly from its source in the Lebanon Mountains.

Close by Tsefat are Mount Canaan, the highest inhabited spot in Israel, and Mount Meiron, Israel's highest point. From here, on a clear day, both the Sea of Galilee to the southeast and the Mediterranean Ocean to the west can be seen. Due to Tsefat's altitude (2,775 feet above sea level) and its cool, invigorating air, the city attracts many visitors and vacationers who find it a favorite summer resort. Over the centuries, many distinguished Hebrew scholars have come to Tsefat, where, in the pleasant surroundings of the Galilean hills and under the inspiration of the beautiful view and the bracing atmosphere, they have produced some of Israel's best literature and some of its most illuminating and penetrating treatises on Hebrew scripture.

The city's name, Safed (in Arabic), can be traced back to the crusader period. However, this was an important inhabited area in the Canaanite era, before Abraham's day. In fact, legend maintains that an ancient cave, which now can be visited at Tsefat, was a place once occupied by Shem, son of Noah. This old cave is named "Beit Hamidrash shel Shem va-Ever." This, in Hebrew means, "The study house of Shem and his great-grandson, Ever." In this cave, allegedly, Shem and Ever studied the Torah (the law), which later was taught to Jacob and, through him, given to his son Joseph.

When Abraham entered the Promised Land, he would have passed through or near the Galilean mountains and probably near the site of Tsefat as he and his party traveled on to Shechem. It was at Shechem that he built his first altar and that he made his first semi-permanent settlement. It was also back to this northern part of the country that he and his descendants came to make this one of their permanent homes.

When Joshua and the Children of Israel entered the Promised Land and conquered it, it is believed that this mountainous area to the north and west of the Sea of Galilee offered effective resistance to the Israelite conquest. The Hittites and the Hivites who lived here were apparently able to continue to hold the valleys and other arable lands, forcing the Israelites to occupy the mountainous areas. According to the scriptures, the reason why these enemies, including the Philistines and the Canaanites, were allowed to remain in the land was to "prove Israel by them,

. . . to know whether they would hearken unto the commandments of the Lord, which he commanded their fathers by the hand of Moses." (Judges 3:1-5.) Later in Old Testament history, according to legend, the body of the prophet Hosea, who died in Babylon, was brought here on a camel and buried in what is now Tsefat's old cemetery.

There are no references in the New Testament placing any of Jesus Christ's activities specifically at or around what is now the city of Tsefat. Nevertheless, Jesus was raised in Galilee and spent most of his life and much of his ministry in this small, confined area. Beyond all reasonable doubt, he was well acquainted with the Galilean mountains and, in all probability, visited the high spots around what is now Tsefat which provide such a beautiful view of all of the surrounding territory.

When one visits this rugged but pleasant area, one senses a strong feeling that Jesus must have walked here. Most of his disciples were selected from the Galilean area. Many of his miracles were performed here, and much of his teaching was given to the people throughout Galilee. After his resurrection, he instructed his disciples and followers to go to Galilee, and he would meet them there. "Then the eleven disciples went away into Galilee, into a mountain where Jesus had appointed them. And when they saw him, they worshipped him. . . ." (Matt. 28:16-17.)

We do not know which mountain in Galilee   **239**

Jesus chose as the one where he would meet his disciples and give them his final instructions. Nevertheless, the highest of these Galilean mountains surround the present city of Tsefat, and it could have been to these, overlooking the valley below and the beautiful Sea of Galilee, that the resurrected Christ came and admonished his disciples to teach all nations, "to observe all things whatsoever I have commanded you: and, lo, I am with you alway, even unto the end of the world." (Matt. 28:20.)

The first historical reference to a city with the actual name of Tsefat was made in the late Middle Ages at the time of the crusaders. When the crusaders occupied Palestine, they fortified themselves on the heights surrounding the present city and called the place Saphet. When the Moslems conquered the country they made this town their capital of the northern district of Palestine and named it Safed.

Tsefat, today, is known as a sacred Hebrew city not only because of its ancient traditions, but also because over the years, since the crusaders' times, many other Jewish rabbis and scholars have sojourned here and have produced important Hebrew literature and some of the most penetrating of the Hebrew scriptures. Many renowned Hebrew writers and historians lived and died here and their tombs attract many visitors.

Tsefat is perched in the Galilean hills 3,000 feet above the Mediterranean and overlooking the Sea of Galilee.
(Photo Courtesy of Israel Government Tourist Office.)

In Jordan–

Jerash

one of the Decapolis cities

"Is there no balm in Gilead; is there no physician there? . . ."
(Jer. 8:22.)

Part of the magnificent ruins at Jerash in Jordan.

Remains of the impressive forum at the head of the street of columns in Jerash.

244

THE ruins of Jerash (Gerasa) are among the most extensive and spectacular in the Middle East.

This magnificent city is located in Jordan territory about 30 miles southeast of the Sea of Galilee and about 35 miles north of Amman on a good paved highway that runs from this capital city of Jordan to Damascus in Syria.

The Jerash ruins are located in the tops of the Gilead Mountains. Until the present road was completed, the area was relatively remote and inaccessible. Consequently, the ruins have not suffered extensively from human desecration and show chiefly only the ravages of weather and time.

Here, today, one can walk by the remains of a beautiful entrance gate and into a large forum surrounded by delicately shaped columns. This forum leads into the "Street of Columns" over 1,000 feet long which is lined on both sides with the remains of 260 Corinthian pillars topped with beautifully carved "capitals" or capstones.

The cobblestones which form the pavement for this avenue still show the worn ruts made by the wheels of countless chariots which, during the Roman period, rode back and forth down the street.

Among the extensive ruins of Jerash, one can visit the remains of once beautiful temples, palaces, shops and magnificent government structures. The whole area is dominated by the remains of what once was the impressive Temple of Artemis, who was the patron goddess of the city and whose temple could be seen and admired for many miles in all directions.

Although the origin and history of Jerash is somewhat vague, reliable evidence indicates that the city may have been built on the ancient site of Ramoth-Gilead. It was near this city, on the banks of the River Jabbock, that Jacob wrestled with the angels and his name was changed to Israel. An Ishmaelite caravan was coming from this area, loaded with spices and with "balm of Gilead," when it met the brothers of Joseph at Dothan. Here the brothers sold Joseph to the caravan which carried him into Egypt.

Ramoth-Gilead was distinguished in that it was one of the six cities of refuge. During the early history of Israel, these cities were sanctuaries into which fugitives could flee and where, if they were accepted into the community, they could reside in safety. David sought refuge here when he was fleeing from the wrath of Absalom. This was the country from which the Prophet Elijah came, and it was here that Elisha anointed Jehu to be king.

Historical reference to the city of Jerash was first recorded by Josephus, who indicated that Theodorsus of Philadelphia took some of his treasures for safekeeping to the temple of Zeus at Jerash.

Alexander Jannaeus, the Jewish ruler (102-76 B.C.), captured Jerash, and it remained in Jewish hands until the advent of the Romans. During the

Roman period the city was greatly enlarged and beautified. It is largely the remains of these ruins which are visible today.

During the early Christian era Jerash was one of the Decapolis cities. The Decapolis was a region encompassing ten cities near and immediately to the east of the Sea of Galilee. According to Pliny, who wrote about this area, these were ancient Greek cities which the Romans allowed to remain Greek in population and government and which were given a trade-free status.

The Decapolis cities attracted a considerable amount of commerce. They were situated on the main trade routes between the lands of the Euphrates to the east, the fertile area of Palestine along the coast of the Mediterranean, and Egypt to the south.

Most of the ten Decapolis cities have vanished without trace. Only three remain as modern communities or as ruins. They are Damascus, Amman (Philadelphia, during Jesus' time) and Jerash.

When Jesus gave his impressive Sermon on the Mount, which included his beautiful Beatitudes, his audience consisted of his disciples and followers from around the area of Galilee, from as far north as Jerusalem and also from the Decapolis.

Matthew recorded this occasion as follows:

"And there followed him great multitudes of people from Galilee, and from Decapolis, and from

Jerusalem, and from Judaea, and from beyond Jordan." (Matt. 4:25.)

Although other references to the Decapolis are found in the New Testament, this area, important during the ministry of the Savior, with its interesting and unusual cities, is all but forgotten today. Much is written about Judea, Samaria, and Galilee, but the area of Decapolis is relatively unknown.

What was the nature of this important area during and prior to the time of Jesus? What were the Decapolis cities and what were their origins? Why did Jesus visit them and perform miracles there?

At the time of Jesus' ministry, the Decapolis was the northern region of Peraea, which was a territory some 15 to 30 miles wide and approximately 85 miles long, east of the Jordan River. The area extended from the Sea of Galilee to the mid-point of the Dead Sea, then known as the Sea of the Plain.

According to Pliny the Younger, the names of these Decapolis cities were Raphana, Scythopolis, Gadara, Hippos, Dion, Pella, Canatha, Damascus, Philadelphia (Ammon), and Gerasa (Jerash).

All of these communities, with the exception of Damascus, were located within the confines of the territory of Decapolis, and some of them were close to the southeastern shores of the Sea of Galilee.

During early Hebrew history, certain cities were **248** designated as places of sanctity and of refuge. Individuals who were being harassed by their enemies or those who had committed crimes, even as serious as murder, could flee to these cities and there find asylum and protection.

As long as they remained in the city of refuge and so long as they abided by the rules and laws established there, they could remain in security. However, if they committed any crimes or in any way violated the city's ordinances, they would be driven out and then become subject to the retribution or mercy of those who were pursuing them.

Prior to the Christian era there were six such cities of refuge throughout Palestine—three in the north and three in the south. We are not sure that all of the Decapolis cities were successors to or expansions of the cities of refuge, but we know that at least one of those in the south was Ramoth in Gilead and, according to Hastings, Ramoth was the earlier name of Gerasa or Jerash.

In view of the fact that Jerash earlier had been one of these refuge cities, it is reasonable to assume that the other Decapolis cities were also places of refuge. At least they were communities of a special nature.

Before, during, and after the Savior's ministry the ten Decapolis cities enjoyed special political privileges granted by Rome since 63 B.C. These were Greek cities, apparently, into which Greek citizens had fled for refuge after the Romans had defeated the Greeks in the conquest of Palestine.

249

Not only were certain tax privileges extended to the inhabitants of these cities, but they were also allowed, virtually, to govern themselves as long as they did not interfere with the over-all Roman rule.

Most of these communities have long since been destroyed and their remains are so scattered or covered by the debris of the centuries that it is impossible to fix their exact original sites. Two of them, however, remain as important Middle Eastern cities. These are Philadelphia, presently Ammon, the capital city of Jordan, and Damascus, the capital of Syria.

The site of another, Gerasa, currently known as Jerash, remains as one of the most impressive ruins in the whole area of the Middle East.

History and origin of Philadelphia, the city of brotherly love, goes back to before the time of Christ. It is recorded that the city was founded and named by Attalus Philadelphus sometime before 138 B.C. The city was situated on the trade route between the fertile valleys of the Euphrates and the important communities along the coast of the Mediterranean. At the time of Jesus' ministry, Philadelphia was a beautiful Greco-Roman city with marble-sculptured, colonnaded buildings and with a spacious amphitheater.

It was a vital trade city with a population primarily Greek and Hebrew. The apostle John, in his book of Revelation, refers to the church in Philadelphia, indicating that the Christians had gained a strong foothold there.

Earlier, in Old Testament times, an interesting historical incident occurred in this area. Approximately 1,000 years before Christ, the great King David was engaged in a war with the Ammonites who had their military headquarters at Rabath-Ammon, which, as indicated, was later renamed Philadelphia.

Damascus is believed to be the oldest continuously inhabited city in the world. The city's origin is lost in antiquity but it flourished around much of Old Testament times. The earliest reference to the city is found in the 14th chapter of Genesis, which describes the battle Abram had with the four kings who had conquered Sodom and Gomorrah and had captured Lot, Abram's brother's son. Abram defeated the four kings and rescued his nephew.

Later, when King David, through conquest, was expanding the boundaries of Israel to their all-time limits, he conquered Damascus. In New Testament times, one of the best known stories involving Damascus is connected with the apostle Paul's conversion.

The ruins of Jerash, which were explored in the early 1930s by the British School of Archaeology in Jerusalem, assisted by Yale University and the American School of Oriental Research in Jerusalem, revealed the remains of what must have been one of the most beautiful cities of pre-Christian times. The ruins are located in the highlands of Gilead, which is the northern-most section of the Decapolis.

The city is approximately 23 miles from Ammon and is the best preserved Palestinian city of Roman times. Josephus states that the city was captured by Alexander Jannaeus in approximately 83 B.C. It was rebuilt by the Romans and later burned by Vespasian's captain.

Even after the ravages of the ages, this magnificent ruin contains the remains of a circular, colonnaded forum, some 300 feet in diameter, from which a well-preserved, paved street leads to a monumental north gate, which was built by Trojan about 100 years after the birth of Jesus.

At the south end of the city, Adrian built a triumphal arch (A.D. 130), the ruins of which still indicate its magnificence. The principal building in the city was the Temple of Artemis, which was constructed over a period of several decades, probably during and immediately after the Savior's ministry.

Remains of the Temple of Artemis which dominate the Jerash ruins.

In Appreciation

D URING their visits in the Middle East, the authors received invaluable assistance from many individuals and the organizations they serve. Sincere appreciation is expressed to United Press International and to those staffers of this organization located in major cities throughout the area who gave unselfishly of their time and assistance. Special appreciation is expressed to Eliav Simon, former UPI Israel bureau chief, and to Raja Elissa, former UPI chief, Jerusalem, Jordan.

Sincerest appreciation is also expressed to the Israel Government Tourist Office for its generous help in arranging and helping the authors in their visits and for assistance in providing photographs. The authors especially wish to express their gratitude to Asher Rahav, director of this office in Beverly Hills, California, who was most helpful and encouraging in the preparation of this book. Also to Perry Rudolph and Jacob Danker then of the Public Relations Department of the Israel Government Tourist Office, who provided the excellent historical-guide service which made the authors' visits so enjoyable and informative.

Most of the chapters in this book appeared originally as articles in the *Church news* of the *Deseret News*. The authors are grateful to the editors of this publication for permission to reproduce this material.

Unless otherwise indicated, all photographs are by the authors.

O. P. R.

C. H. R.

Additional Biblical References

Jerusalem

Genesis 22:2; Joshua 10:1-25; Judges 1, 19; 2 Kings 18; 19; 20; 24; 25; Isaiah 2:3; 44:24-28; Psalms 110:4; 2 Samuel 5:6-16; 6:1-18; Matthew 27; Mark 15; Luke 23.

Acre

Joshua 19:24-31 (area given to Asher); Judges 1:31, 32.

Ashkelon

Joshua 13:3 (area still to be conquered); Judges 1:17-19 (Judah conquers it); 14:19 (Samson smites the Philistines. For prophets' warnings, see Amos 1:8: Zephaniah 2:4, 7; Jeremiah 25:20; 47:6, 7.

Beersheba

Genesis 21 (Hagar cast out); 28 (Jacob leaves for Haran); 46 (Israel returns); 1 Kings 19:1-8 (Elijah flees here from Jezebel).

Caesarea

Acts 8, 10, 21, 23, 25, 26.

Caesarea Philippi

Matthew 16; Mark 8:27; 9:10; Luke 9:18-36.

Capernaum

Matthew 4:13-17 (Jesus lived here); 8:5, 15-17; 9:1-8, 18-26; 13; Mark 1:21-23; 2:12; 9:33; 15:1-20; Luke 4:31-38; John 4:46; 6:59.

Gath

Joshua 11:22-23 (Joshua takes the land); 1 Samuel 5:8-10 (Arc of the Covenant brought here); 1 Samuel 17 (David and Goliath); 21:10 (David flees here); 1 Chronicles 18:1 (David captures it).

Hazor

Joshua 11; Judges 4. (Recently a bone handle has been found in the excavations at Hazor. This artifact has engraved upon it a date palm protected by a seraph and cherubin and the flaming sword. See Genesis 3:24.) Solomin had chariots here (see 1 Kings 9).

Hebron

Genesis 15, 16, 17, 23, 25, 35, 37, 49, 50; 2 Samuel 2, 3, 5; 1 Kings 2:11; 2 Samuel 15 (Absalom's conspiracy).

Jericho

Deuteronomy 34 (Moses looks over the land); Numbers 26; Joshua 1:7; 2; 10; 16; 18; 2 Kings 25:5-7 (Zedekiah's sons killed here).

Joppa

Joshua 19:46; Ezra 3:7; 2 Chronicles 2:16; Acts 9; 10; 11.

Megiddo

Joshua 12:7, 21; 17:11; 1 Chronicles 7:29; Judges 5:19, 20; 1 Kings 9:15; 2 Kings 9:27; 23:29; 35:22; Zechariah 14:2, 3.

Nazareth

Isaiah 7:14; Luke 1:26-38; 2:1-7; Mark 9; Luke 4:16-30; Matthew 13:53-58.

Sebaste

1 Kings 16:23-28; 22:37; Amos 6:1; 2 Kings 1; 5; 17; 18.

Sodom and Gomorrah

Genesis 19; Deuteronomy 29:23; Matthew 10:15; Revelation 11:8.

Tsefat

Matthew 5:14 (believed to have been referred to by Jesus when he said, "A city that is set on a hill cannot be hid").

Index